Not a Toy, but a Tool

Further Praise for *Not a Toy, but a Tool*

"*Note at Toy, but a Tool* provides educators with a wide variety of available resources to enhance their classroom instruction when using iPads. Carrie Thornthwaite has broken the book into sections that help teachers easily access apps that are appropriate and specific to their instructional needs. As a reading specialist, I am always looking for high-quality apps that can be used to help students reach their highest reading potential. The organization of the book allows me to easily find the apps that I need for my students. The research that has already been done by the author will help me manage my time when using iPads in the classroom. I've been using iPads for a couple years, but now, with this information, I can integrate iPads more effectively into my classroom instruction."

— **Laurie Love**, reading specialist at Columbia Academy, Columbia, TN

"As a high school history teacher, I find this an extremely valuable book. As a geography and history teacher, I particularly liked the apps in chapter 5. Some of the apps provide primary sources, which is important in implementing Common Core. The other apps have given me innumerable ideas for lessons that I can use in my classes. I highly recommend this book for use by any classroom teacher."

— **Amanda Elmore**, Hendersonville High School, Sumner County, TN

"Talk about iPads, this book itself is a learning tool that can be accessed by students, parents, and teachers alike. Students can be encouraged to reinforce their classroom learning simply by using the apps that are discussed here. Teachers will be released from hours of searching for appropriate learning tools to enrich or remediate their lessons. Parents will be able to choose apps that correlate with their child's academic curriculum. Students will gladly reinforce their studies because using the iPad does not seem like work. As a former teacher and a current mentor of novice and pre-service teachers, I applaud Dr. Thornthwaite's research."

— **Bonnie S. Barker**, M.Ed., Tennessee Academic Specialist, adjunct professor and former high school mathematics and English teacher

"Thornthwaite is obviously very educated and knowledgeable about iPads. As a kindergarten teacher, I found many of the apps in the elementary sections to be very helpful. I downloaded some and my kids love them. I have been using iPads in my classroom daily to assist me with enforcing and mastering skills that we are learning every day. It is great to have this book as a resource for broadening the activities that I've been using. The apps allow me to adapt my instruction to the many different learning needs of my students. With the help of this book, I have been able to teach and reach students that otherwise were having difficulty grasping and understanding new skills. With many of the apps, I've been able to break the skills down in a fun game type way of learning."

—**Shelley Hatfield Cash**, kindergarten teacher,
Robbins Elementary School, Scott County, Robbins, TN

Not a Toy, but a Tool

An Educator's Guide for Understanding and Using iPads

Carrie Thornthwaite

ROWMAN & LITTLEFIELD
Lanham • Boulder • New York • Toronto • Plymouth, UK

Published by Rowman & Littlefield
4501 Forbes Boulevard, Suite 200, Lanham, Maryland 20706
www.rowman.com

10 Thornbury Road, Plymouth PL6 7PP, United Kingdom

British Library Cataloguing in Publication Information Available

Library of Congress Cataloging-in-Publication Data

Thornthwaite, Carrie.
  Not a toy, but a tool : an educator's guide for understanding and using iPads / Carrie
Thornthwaite.
    pages cm
  Includes bibliographical references and index.
  ISBN 978-1-4758-0939-8 (cloth : alk. paper) — ISBN 978-1-4758-0940-4 (pbk. :
alk. paper) — ISBN 978-1-4758-0941-1 (electronic : alk. paper) 1. Computer-assisted
instruction. 2. iPad (Computer) 3. Tablet computers. I. Title.
  LB1028.5.T515 2014
  371.33'4—dc23

                                                                    2013046509

♾™ The paper used in this publication meets the minimum requirements of
American National Standard for Information Sciences—Permanence of Paper
for Printed Library Materials, ANSI/NISO Z39.48-1992.

Printed in the United States of America

Contents

—∞—

Preface

iPads are powerful tools for engaging students, encouraging creativity, stimulating critical thinking, and making significant strides in learning. I have come to that conclusion after three years of working with iPads in a variety of academic settings. Yet research shows that even among educators, there exists a misunderstanding about the potential that iPads can offer, especially for teaching and learning. For example, in my travels, I visited one school where the teachers informed me that three carts of iPads were available for their use. One person at the school had been designated as the caretaker of those iPads, so I asked if I could talk with her.

When I met the caretaker, I introduced myself and then asked her what apps the teachers were using. I was stunned when she answered, "None." Immediately, I asked, "Why?" Her reply came quickly, "They cost too much." Of course, I assured her that there are vast numbers of free apps. She then replied, "You don't understand. Our students want Microsoft Word and it doesn't have that."

When I tried to explain that iPads were designed to function entirely differently from computers, she interrupted, "I know. That's why our students don't like them." Another teacher at the school told me that students use the iPads only "to look up stuff on the Internet." I left their school that day unconvinced that the students did not like iPads. The problem was that the woman who took care of the iPads viewed them as merely highly ineffective computers. Some educators retain a total lack of understanding about the incredible potential of this device. How tragic!

This book and a companion book have been written so that principals, media specialists, teachers, and parents can understand the tremendous value provided by iPads in the field of education. The information in both books covers all subject areas and grade levels in order to share the reasons for my convictions and to recommend a large collection of apps that are perfect for enhancing teaching and learning in today's classrooms. This book also addresses the issue of what exactly an iPad is. In addition, both books provide information for users of other tablets. That is explained further in the introduction of this book.

My passion for the effectiveness of iPads comes after thirty years of serving the profession as an educator. I have been teaching at the university level for sixteen years, and, previously, I taught physics and mathematics at the high school level. The situation today of some educators resisting the use of iPads reminds me of the skepticism that many teachers held, a few decades back, concerning the use of the Internet.

Back in 1991, I was the first teacher at the urban high school where I taught to have Internet access through a phone line to one of my classroom computers. After lunch, I remember hearing a rare sound of the students running down the hall to try to be the first to reach my classroom. The students ran to get there in order to read the responses sent from students in other schools from around the world about the quality of water in their various areas.

I could have had my students read a textbook about water quality. However, the new technology of emails was far more engaging. My students learned substantially more about water quality through that project than would have been possible from class lectures or textbooks. Today, I believe that students are running to iPad-equipped classrooms! With the resources provided in these two books, teachers can enjoy the experience of having students excited to use the iPad and engaged in achieving an understanding of key topics.

Acknowledgments

To my guides . . .

In my role as teacher/professor, I have always tried to hold as much as possible to the adage of being a "guide on the side" rather than the uninspiring lecturer acting as a "sage on the stage." As I reflect over more than a year that was needed to assimilate the information that is contained in the book, I realize that the final product would not have been possible without many guides on the side who gently helped to move me through the process of publication. My gratitude to each of these folks cannot be overstated.

Above all, my deepest gratitude goes to my dear friend Melanie Crotty, who served for many years as the reference librarian at Burlington County Library, New Jersey. Melanie read every page of the prepublication manuscript, editing each chapter with expertise and diligence. In addition, we discussed together many aspects of ways to improve the chapters.

Immense gratitude should also be expressed to Phillip Brackett, who serves as the technology specialist at Lipscomb University's Information Technology Center. Phillip read and edited the first few chapters; additionally, he served as my technical expert on iPads.

My friend Emily Wilson-Orzechowski read the chapter on apps for the English classroom. She spent considerable time editing and adding suggestions. As a physics major, writing was never my first love. Emily, however, is the former writing center coordinator at Hartwick College, Oneonta, New York. Her expertise was immensely helpful; the notes that she provided assisted me with my writing throughout the remainder of the book.

My colleague Nina Morel, codirector of Lipscomb's College of Education master's program, was tremendously helpful in guiding me through the first steps of starting toward publication. Nina read and edited the first chapter. As a published author, her advice gave me considerable insight into the struggles that I might face.

Jesse Savage, a principal at Lipscomb Academy, was extremely kind in providing advice and time. Through early discussions, Jesse helped me understand the difficulties inherent with using shared iPads. After using carts of iPads for several years, Lipscomb Academy has now begun a 1-to-1 iPad initiative, thanks to the tremendous work of Mr. Savage. He allowed me to attend professional development sessions, which he taught for his teachers, concerning classroom uses of the iPad and evaluated one of the chapters from this book.

Having considerable experience in both secondary and postsecondary education, I had clear ideas of how iPads could enhance instruction in those classrooms. However, originally I had some difficulty envisioning the use of the iPad in elementary classrooms. Then I met Timothy Carey, the media arts teacher for K–4 students at Henry C. Maxwell Elementary in Antioch, Tennesee. I was able to observe him using the iPad as an art-making tool with apps such as Brushes, Puppet Pals HD, and Faces iMake. Even with kindergarten students, the iPads served as great tools. I appreciate Mr. Carey's willingness to let me observe his classes and to discuss with him the insights he had on how to successfully use iPads with very young children.

My gratitude also goes to others who helped me more indirectly. Those include my husband, other family members, my students, my colleagues, and my church family. Finally, I'd like to dedicate this book to my precious two-year-old grandson, Thomas Rex Miller, who is already adept at using his iPad for learning

Introduction

This book is part of a two-book set, which delves into the tremendous value that iPads can provide to educators. This book focuses primarily on iPads for two reasons: (1) apps tend to hit the iPad market first, then only later some may be adapted for other tablets, and (2) the quantity of educational apps on iPad far exceeds the number available on other tablets. However, in recognition that some educators and students may have access to other devices, there is a note provided in these books, by each app's description, whether it is "also available on Android." Tablet owners can check later to see whether additional apps become available on their devices.

Both books of this set start with a chapter based on research; all subsequent chapters focus on apps that are appropriate for specific subject areas. Chapter 1 of this book starts by clarifying the question "What is an iPad?" As the title of the book reflects, many believe that the device is purely a toy, but considerable evidence exists to support the contention that the iPad is a valuable tool for engaging students and promoting learning.

Chapter 1 also shares ten specific reasons iPads are valuable instructional tools, well worth the investment. The chapter closes with examples of how the iPad can be used. The ideal is to have a one-to-one classroom, where the teacher and each student own individual iPads. However, different techniques can be used in which iPads can be equally valuable when using classroom sets. Less ideal, but still valuable, are the scenarios where the teacher has only a small number of iPads. Even when there is only a single iPad in a classroom, techniques are available for engaging students and promoting learning with the single device.

The remaining chapters of this book focus on sharing information about specific apps. Chapters 2 and 3 provide information on twenty-three apps that can be used across all subject areas. The last three chapters offer descriptions of subject-specific apps that are appropriate for use in the humanities. Chapter 4 focuses on sixteen apps appropriate for the English classroom; chapter 5 describes fifteen apps that can be used in history classes; and chapter 6 deals with foreign language apps. In chapters 4 and 5, the apps are sorted with five for elementary-, five for middle-, and five for high school–level classrooms. In chapter 6, the apps are sorted according to the specific language.

Within the various sections and also at the end of each chapter, websites are listed that provide additional information. Also, additional apps may be recommended. Finally, at the end of each chapter, there is a list of apps that are described in other areas of the two-book set. For example, at the end of the English chapter (chapter 4), an app is listed named PrepZilla Study with Friends Game. That app is discussed fully in a chapter on mathematics that is found in *The Deuce and a Half iPad: An Educator's Guide for Bringing Discovery, Engagement, Understanding, and Creativity into Education.* However, it has features that provide value to both the mathematics and English classrooms.

Throughout the book, two criteria were used for selecting apps: high quality and low cost. Each app in these books has gained high ratings from iTunes, as well as from other sources. Concerning cost, apps that were free or less than $1.99 were originally selected. In a couple of cases, a $2.99 app has been retained because the quality of the app warranted the additional expense.

Concerning the length of the descriptions for each app, they are primarily overviews. With the limited space, descriptions could not possibly include every bell and whistle within each app. However, the descriptions provide enough information so that readers will be able to make informed decisions concerning the selection of apps from an immense pool of apps. The instructions in this book also provide readers with an understanding of the key features. In addition, attention is drawn to nearly hidden links within particular apps that open up entirely new areas. Of course, with new updates, even more features may become available, so readers are encouraged to pay attention to updates as they become available.

Another question may arise concerning the durability of the apps that are covered in this text. There is, in fact, a steady flow of apps that do not enjoy a very long survival, although those are generally *not* the highly rated apps.

Compared to the more than 900,000 apps that are currently available, there may be as many as 400,000 inactive apps that can no longer be downloaded. However, those apps are nearly always the ones with low ratings; most likely they were dropped, as they could not find a sufficient market amid the immense collection of apps.

Two other change scenarios are more likely: (1) an occasional increase in price and (2) the appearance of powerful, newly designed apps that deserve recognition. The fear about the price increases is also exaggerated. In fact, while increases do occur, recent trends actually show an increase in the percentage of apps that are free. The appearance of a stellar new app that might trump all previous apps in a particular subject area indeed may occur.

To address any occurrences of dropped apps, increases in prices, and the appearance of new apps, a wiki has been created to alert readers about any of those changes. The wiki will be updated regularly to share (1) the status of all apps that are covered in this book and (2) the appearance of new apps that show promise for specific areas. After the introductory home page, the wiki pages are sorted by subject area. A discussion area at the bottom of each subject-area page allows members to comment on existing apps and/or to add comments about newly discovered apps.

Finally, readers should be aware that some of the websites that are listed throughout the book may not be available as months pass. Those websites are included only as additional resources or references. If a website disappears that had important instructive information, a note will be made on the wiki, and an alternate site will be suggested.

The wiki is private, but readers can request to be a member of this Wikispaces wiki by sending an email to the author at carrie.thornthwaite@ lipscomb.edu. In the message, please include specifically where the text was purchased. Any comments about the book will also be appreciated.

Private wiki iPads for Tools not Toys: ipad4atoolnottoy.wikispaces.com

More information on recent trends with apps:

Available apps 2013: en.wikipedia.org/wiki/App_Store_%28iOS%29

2012 Statistics: 148apps.biz/app-store-metrics/

Trend for free apps continues to rise: appadvice.com/appnn/2013/07/number -of-free-apps-in-the-app-store-continues-to-rise

—⟶⟶⟶—

CHAPTER ONE

Not a Toy, but a Tool!

Introduction

iPads are powerful tools for engaging students, encouraging creativity, stimulating critical thinking, and making significant strides in learning. Yet that fact is in stark contrast to the findings from a July 2011 survey by Citigroup, which canvassed 1,800 consumers from the United States, the United Kingdom, and China. Tragically, 62 percent of the respondents selected that their reason for purchasing an iPad was to use the device "as a new toy/gadget." Only 18 percent selected "for work" (Kafka, 2011).

Those results reflect a misunderstanding about the potential that iPads can offer—especially for teaching and learning. This book has been written for principals, media specialists, teachers and parents. The information covers all subject areas and grade levels in order to share the reasons for educators to use iPads and to recommend a large collection of apps that are perfect for enhancing teaching and learning in today's classrooms.

In this two-book set, over two hundred apps are discussed; each has the potential for enhancing learning. Chapters 2 and 3 in the book cover apps that can be used across all subject areas. Then chapter 4 and all the following chapters introduce apps that were designed for use in specific subject areas. However, before beginning a discussion of the apps, several issues concerning iPads need to be clarified. That is the purpose of this first chapter.

The inspiration to spread the word about iPads to a larger audience came after the realization that many educators still fail to understand what an iPad is. How can you effectively use a device if you don't know what it is? Also, teachers should be able to explain to their principals and, likewise, principals to their superintendents the reasons for using an iPad. The chapter discusses ten very valid reasons for using this device. Finally, the chapter closes with descriptions of the variety of ways that an iPad can be used. Using it in only one way would be shortchanging its potential. So, in short, this first chapter will address the following key questions:

- *What* exactly is an iPad—a toy, a mini computer, or something entirely different?
- *Why* should educators want to use this device (ten reasons)?
- *How* can it be used in today's schools? Is there flexibility in the way that it is used?

An understanding of the answers to those questions is essential before any educator should endeavor to advocate for the use of iPads in today's schools. All educators should find the device valuable and thus become knowledgeable advocates for iPads. If any readers had hoped to find details here about how to turn the iPad on and get started with using it, they would need to look elsewhere. There are plenty of books already available covering those topics. This book exclusively focuses on how to effectively use the iPad in schools and how to become a knowledgeable proponent for its use.

What Exactly Is an iPad?

The first generation iPad hit the market in January 2010, with Steve Jobs describing it as "a truly magical and revolutionary product" (Suffer & Gross, 2010). Being "magical and revolutionary" may spark initial sales, but long-term success requires that the device meets a more concrete need. Two and a half years after its introduction, CNET news reported, "Apple's iPad is outpacing traditional PCs in sales to students and schools for the first time ever" (Kerr, 2012). Teachers across the nation are seeking out information about iPads. Early indications on more than half a dozen studies do indicate that iPads improve learning (Baugh, 2012).

Obviously, a significant number of teachers and administrators must believe that the iPad deserves to play a meaningful role in today's classrooms. Unfortunately, though, as mentioned in both the preface of this book and in the opening paragraph of this chapter, some educators still do not understand the true functionality and potential of iPads.

Consider the question "Is an iPad just another computer?" In April 2010, an article in *Wired* magazine described the iPad as "a computer that people won't think of as a computer" (Levy, 2010). That same month, another article in *Consumer Electronics* asked the question "Is the Apple iPad a computer or an entertainment device?" (Cherry, 2010). Ackerman (2010) offered three options with a similar question: "Is the iPad a 'real' computer, a big portable media player, or something brand new?"

Of course, some arguments can be made for the iPad being a computer. Computers are generally understood to be electronic devices that process, store, and retrieve data. Obviously, the iPad does have those capabilities. Furthermore, just like a computer, you can print wirelessly and even use an external keyboard. Also, the iPad, as does every computer, has an operating system (OS). The OS is the software that supports the basic functions of both devices. However, the operating system of an iPad cannot match the capabilities of a computer's OS.

So, although the iPad has some of the basic features of a computer, it still pales in comparison to today's models. Does that matter? Even Steve Jobs acknowledged that the iPad was NOT a computer, in the fullest sense of the word (Rosoff, 2011). It was never intended to replace a computer. Now, you can type a paper on an iPad, but that doesn't mean you should.

Apple has never suggested that the iPad is just another computer, nor is it just an entertainment device, despite the fact that it does have features that can be very entertaining. Similarly, it is not just "a big portable media player," although it does play media quite well. The iPad is quite simply a unique device . . . a new product.

Why Should Educators Want to Use iPads?

This section can help any educator who has to argue a case for wanting an iPad. So what is the value of an iPad, and why exactly should an administrator or a grant committee approve turning over funds for its purchase? Ideally, every teacher in every class should have access to, at the very least, the following three devices: a computer, a large monitor, and an iPad. Each of those, along with the associated connectivity and basic software, is essential for supporting a modern classroom with full access to digital resources.

Why should iPads be considered "essential," above a second computer or a myriad of other technology devices? There are at least ten reasons that support the value of these devices. The reasons are described below in an order of generally increasing significance, reflecting a gradual flow toward the most critical issues.

First, consider its *convenience*, or *maneuverability*. At 1.44 pounds for the iPad or .86 pounds for the mini, this device is smaller and less than half the weight of the smallest laptop. In a classroom setting, an iPad is even easier to carry around than a textbook. One research study from Reed College in Portland, Oregon, determined that "[b]ecause the iPad made it easy for the students to have all their course readings with them at all times, they found that they read and reviewed the materials more frequently than they would otherwise" (Marmarelli & Ringle, 2011). Consequently, the potential exists for a positive correlation between the use of iPads and student learning.

Next, in this list of ten reasons for using iPads, is the brief *start-up time*. In classrooms, the slow start-up time of most computers can be distracting. Educators are frequently frustrated with the time wasted while a computer takes up to several minutes to boot up. iPads have virtually instantaneous start-up times, so wait time is never an issue. In addition to that, crashes are very rare with iPads, so the need to reboot is seldom an issue.

The third advantage of the iPad hardware is its *durability*, or *robustness*, which covers both the iPad battery and its operating system. The battery of an iPad can last for ten hours before needing to be recharged. In other words, a fully charged iPad will last through an entire school day and then even have time left over for after-school tutoring sessions! Compare that to computers! One online article stated that "the battery life of laptops can range wildly: We've seen some systems push 7 hours, and others have trouble even clearing an hour and a half." (Ackerman, 2010). Recharging iPads can be done every night.

In fact, a healthy battery will be maintained by letting it run down to below 20 percent before recharging. Of course, there's no guarantee that a device will always last the full ten hours. That time depends on a lot of factors. One tip that will lengthen the life of a battery is to turn off the Wi-Fi feature if you don't need it. An easy way to do that is to simply go to Settings and turn on the Airplane mode. Frequently, when students are working with specific apps, there is no need to be connected to the Internet. Another tip would be to decrease the brightness. In fact, a Google search for "extending the battery life of an iPad" will provide several other helpful hints.

Concerning the operating system, "[I]t is almost impossible to damage the operating system or get it infected with viruses or malware" (Pawlowski, 2012). As another author summarized:

> The iPad isn't 100% rock-solid; apps do crash from time to time, and I encounter occasional glitches I can solve with a reboot. But in my experience, it's far less susceptible to odd behavior than any conventional computer. The more reliable the device, the more time I can spend doing whatever I'm trying to do. (McCracken, 2012)

The *versatility* of iPads is a huge advantage. This fourth advantage brings to mind the words of Alice, as she wandered through Wonderland: "I'm never sure what I'm going to be, from one minute to another" (Carroll, 1946, p. 61). One minute, a teacher might use an iPad as a movie player to show an important video on the rule of the Tudors in England. In the next classroom, a French or ELL teacher might be using an iPad as a voice recorder to help students improve their pronunciation. A math teacher might be using her iPad like a document camera or whiteboard, asking her students to write in the next step in solving a math problem.

Down the street, at a university, a professor could be using an iPad as a camera to generate a video for each education major teaching his or her first class. The immense number of apps allows for this wide range of activities. In September 2012, Apple bragged that their App Stores hosted over 700,000 apps, with 250,000 of those specifically targeted for iPads (Etherington, 2012). This versatility of apps will be apparent throughout the descriptions in this book.

Some might consider this fifth advantage as the most important . . . that of *cost*. From its introduction in 2010 through the initiation of the fourth-generation iPad, the cost has remained steady at $499 for the 16 GB Wi-Fi model to $829 for the 64 GB Wi-Fi + 4G model. The vast majority of school systems have stayed with the 16 GB model, allowing individuals to select the higher levels at an increased fee.

That is far cheaper than, for example, a MacBook Pro at $1,199 (retail) or most PCs that range from $700 to $2,000. If funds are limited, as they usually are in education, then purchasing iPads would be a far more frugal investment compared to buying other technology devices.

For the sixth advantage, consider the huge advantage of eBooks! One online article, titled "Why Your iPad Is Almost Always The Cheapest Way To Get Your Textbooks," compared the costs of regular new or used textbooks, rented textbooks, and e-textbooks. For a typical student, the author found that eBooks, on average, saved $163.88 per semester over renting and $355.13 over buying (Heine, 2012).

The primary disadvantage, so far, is that those e-textbooks are much more readily available in some subjects and for some grade levels than in others. The skyrocketing sales of eBooks have not impacted the e-textbook market as strongly. However, more and more publishers are coming on board with expanding numbers of available e-textbooks. In 2011, one researcher estimated that "electronic textbooks will generate $267.3 million this year in sales in the United States. That is a rise of 44.3 percent over last year" (Schuetze, 2011).

Furthermore, the e-textbooks that do exist are very impressive with their capabilities of being able to:

- Directly link to audio and video files
- Easily search for related information
- Allow students to more easily and neatly write notes in the margins and highlight important areas of the text
- Easily copy and paste text into note files or for purposes of citation
- Easily share sections with colleagues for discussion purposes

A recent article in *The Chronicle of Higher Education* announced that "five universities announced plans to try bulk purchasing of e-textbooks" through a partnership with McGraw-Hill (Young, 2012). With the cost savings and the increased capacities, e-textbook sales could easily begin to expand exponentially in future years.

The seventh advantage that iPads provide may, at first, seem surprising. That is, the *projection capability*. Of course, projectors have been hooked up to classroom computers since the 1990s. However, computers are typically tethered to a projector in a way that restricts maneuverability. Remotes do allow presenters to move around the room but not with the computer in hand, only with a remote, whereas, for the iPad, either software or a couple small pieces of hardware allow the teacher to walk around the classroom and hand the iPad to a student, who can then solve a problem, select an answer, or make other changes to the iPad that can then be observed on the screen by the whole class.

That flexibility far exceeds the capabilities of a computer, even a laptop. Currently, two software products allow for wireless projecting from iPads. The Reflection app (www.reflectionapp.com/) costs $14.99 for single seat or $49.99 for 5-seat licenses. The software is simply downloaded to either a Mac or PC. Then, in the Settings area of the iPad, users click on Bluetooth and then click on the signal from the computer. Airserver (www.airserverapp.com/) also provides this service, with prices ranging from free (for a 7-day trial) to $59.99 (for 15 licenses).

Another option, although a bit more expensive at approximately $99, is to purchase an Apple TV. An additional $20 may be needed for a video converter if that has not been previously purchased. Those two pieces of hardware will allow mirroring of the iPad in any room that has access to Wi-Fi. The advantage of using the more expensive device is that the Apple TV can be moved to any computer seamlessly. The software is restricted to one or a limited number of computers. For teachers who teach in multiple classrooms or for educators who travel and do a lot of presentations, the Apple TV is preferable.

The eighth reason is that the iPad *stimulates creativity*. This is also an issue of paramount importance. In 2006, Sir Ken Robinson grabbed international attention with his now famous speech titled "Do Schools Kill Creativity?" (TEDxTalks, 2007). In that talk, presented at the TED Conference, as well as in multiple writings, Robinson's passion has been sharing his belief that children are inherently creative. Yet, schools, albeit unintentionally, discourage creativity by overemphasizing memorization and always expecting predetermined answers.

In his book *Out of Our Minds*, Robinson writes, "New technologies are revolutionizing the nature of work everywhere. . . . New forms of work rely increasingly on high levels of specialist knowledge, and on creativity and innovation" (Robinson, 2011, p. 25). In other words, Robinson believes that children are born with the innate ability to be creative, but then schools gradually stifle that creativity. After more than a decade of trudging through our schools, the students graduate only to discover that businesses are expecting them to once again be creative and "think outside the box."

In fact, an article posted on Bloomberg Businessweek reported that "[a]ccording to a new survey of 1,500 chief executives conducted by IBM's Institute for Business Value (IBM), CEOs identify 'creativity' as the most important leadership competency for the successful enterprise of the future" (2010). If that is the case, then schools do indeed need to address this issue by somehow stimulating and encouraging creativity in the classroom. Within a few months of the release of the initial iPad, Computerworld posted an article titled "Why the iPad is a creativity machine." (Elgan, 2010). The iPad clearly has the ability to nourish student creativity.

The final two most important reasons for using iPads could easily be considered to go hand in hand: *engaging students* and *facilitating learning*. One online article states, "The iPad engages students in ways that no piece of school or classroom technology has ever done" (Faas, 2012). Suddenly, classroom management is a nonissue. Positive results are also coming out of university studies.

At Notre Dame, one study found that a "statistically significant proportion of students felt the iPad made class more interesting, encouraged exploration of additional topics, provided functions and tools not possible with a textbook and helped them more effectively manage their time" (Chapla, 2011).

Another study, at Abilene Christian University in Texas, compared the access time that members of a microeconomics class spent on their course's learning management system (LMS) (Blackboard). One group of students was accessing the LMS with laptops and the other with iPads. The study found that students using iPads had an "increased engagement and frequency of access compared to students using a laptop" (Shepherd & Reeves, 2011).

Now consider this very important question: "Do iPads *enhance learning?*" This is undoubtedly the most important reason for bringing iPads into the classroom. The most critical expectation for any teacher is to maximize the amount of learning taking place in his or her classroom. The primary mission of any school should be to enhance the degree of learning acquired by their students.

Of course, if students are engaged in a lesson, as described in the previous paragraph, then, in all likelihood, substantial learning is going on. Teachers can feel an incredible reward by being able to stand back and simply watch their students suddenly experience the proverbial "ah, ha!" moment. By discovering something, students expanded their level of understanding. Mark Van Doren (1944) was right on target when he said, "The art of teaching is the art of assisting discovery."

Students will be far more likely to reach a discovery if they have a tool or tools to assist them. Science teachers, for example, can lecture for days on the topic of velocity and acceleration. They can even provide students with the equation of acceleration = velocity/time. However, little understanding will go on until the students start using their hands. Give the students toy cars to run down ramps and battery-operated tractors that chug along at a constant speed. With sensors and stopwatches, students collect data. Suddenly there are sparks of understanding!

Where lectures fail, the relationship between velocity and acceleration can become clear to students with the hands-on activities. Today, the App Store provides stopwatches and graphical analysis apps that can help bring even more accurate results with such experiments. The iPad brings understanding by allowing students to engage in a vast array of hands-on activities. And that applies to all subjects, not just to science.

Almost immediately after the release of the iPad, researchers began to develop pilot projects that would prove or disprove that iPads could enhance learning. However, many of those studies are still ongoing. Since iPads were first issued in 2010, there has been time for only a limited number of longitudinal studies. A few results began to appear in 2011 and 2012. The next four paragraphs indicate positive results from studies done at the elementary, middle, and high school, as well as university, levels.

A study conducted by the University of Southern California followed 122 *elementary* students as they worked with the app Motion Math. Although the results of that study were specific to only one app, it is representative of thousands of well-designed apps that are available to educators. Some key findings, listed in the executive summary of the study, included (1) children's fractions test scores improved an average of over 15 percent, (2) children's self-efficacy for fractions and their liking of fractions each improved an average of 10 percent, and (3) all participants rated Motion Math as fun (Riconscente, 2012, p. 1).

Houghton Mifflin conducted a study with *middle school* students. The company was testing the effectiveness of their iPad algebra app at Amelia Earhart Middle School in Riverside, California. Students were randomly selected to use the app and then compared to a control group. "The study showed that 78 percent of students who used the HMH algebra iPad app scored 'proficient' or 'advanced' on the California Standards Test, compared to 59 percent of students who used the textbook version." The study also indicated that the students showed an increase in their interest in algebra (Barseghian, 2012).

Certainly, student interest, engagement, and learning are all closely linked. A University of Minnesota study followed a *secondary school* that had recently purchased 300 iPads. The devices were given to students for classroom use only. Hwang (2012) reported, "[S]tudents were empowered to learn on their own. Students could shift their role from passive receivers of knowledge to producers of knowledge." Isn't that the way every classroom should be?

Finally, a study from Trinity College in Australia followed groups of *college students* who were issued iPads for use in any way that they found helpful. The academic achievements of those students were compared with the achievements of students who had not had the use of an iPad. The results showed that the "iPad students achieved the highest individual scores" compared to their control group (Jennings, 2012).

All four of those reports indicate a positive relationship between the classroom uses of iPads and the increased learning of the students. In summary, the "Why Should Teachers Want to Use iPads?" section covered the following ten reasons:

1. Facilitate learning
2. Engage students
3. Stimulate creativity
4. Projection capabilities
5. eBooks
6. Cost
7. Versatility
8. Durability
9. Start-up time
10. Convenience

Each one of those items reflects a very positive and valid reason for bringing iPads into the classroom. On the other hand, are there some negatives with iPads? Of course! Are there some hurdles that will need to be overcome? Absolutely! One Google search on "iPad cons" brought up a full page of pros and con sites. However, most of those were written in 2010 concerning the first iPad, and many issues, such as no camera and set-up time, were addressed with the more recent iPads. Some problems do still remain.

For example, issues related to sharing iPads exist and will be discussed later in this chapter. Also, the iPad's inability to work with Adobe's Flash and Javascript remains one of the biggest criticisms. Of course, the one-finger typing on the pop-up keyboard seems awkward, especially to new users. There are keyboards for iPads, but the additional expense associated with the purchase of large quantities of those keyboards makes that option not very feasible for schools. All told, the positive reasons win out, far and away above any negatives. The hurdles that do exist are well worth any struggle to overcome.

How Can an iPad Be Used in the Classroom?

There is not a blanket technique, nor is there a single step-by-step approach for using iPads in the classroom. Rather, the words from the famous love poem come to mind: "Let me count the ways" (Browning, 1850). However, merely enumerating the various techniques for using iPads would generate an unmanageably long list. Considering the fact that there are thousands of apps and, with a bit of creativity, each app can be used in a wide variety of ways, then one could rightly say that a million or more different ways are available for using an iPad in the classroom.

Add to that the fact that hundreds of apps are being created every day so the possibilities continue to grow. In an effort to organize this section a bit, the techniques are divided into four different scenarios with each being based on the number of available iPads. Obviously, the ideal scenario would be to have the teacher with his or her own iPad and each of the students possessing her or his own personal iPad. This scenario has received the most media attention and is generally called a one-to-one initiative.

The next scenario occurs when schools are either unwilling or unable to initiate the one-to-one option, but they jump into the world of iPads by investing first in several classroom sets of iPads. Next, there may be a situation where a school or classroom has only a few iPads. Finally, the very common case exists where a teacher has his or her own iPad, but there are few or none available for the students. In all four of those cases, the iPad can bring creativity, engagement, and enhancement of learning to the classroom.

One-to-One Initiatives

The vast majority of the articles on the Internet that relate to iPad usage in schools are actually discussing one-to-one initiatives (aka 1:1 initiatives). In 2011, *U.S. News & World Report* reported, "With most schools back in session, students in about 600 districts nationwide will return with a new piece of tech: their own personal Apple iPad" (Koebler, 2011). Presumably, the number of involved districts will continue to grow, at least over the next several years. In October 2012, seven months after the release of the iPad 3, a Google search for "iPad 1:1 initiatives" brought up seventy-one pages with links to one-to-one initiatives for iPads.

Obviously, there has been a proliferation of iPad initiatives across the country. The ideal remains for every student to have his or her own iPad to take to every class and then also to have access to the device while at home. However, care must be taken with any such comprehensive initiative. Just acquiring the funds for a program does not always assure success. Based on extensive readings and discussions with those who have already initiated these programs, the advice appears to focus on five major areas:

1. Sharing the vision
2. Assuring system setup
3. Arranging for security and maintenance
4. Providing ongoing training
5. Welcoming flexibility

Sharing the vision must start with great leadership. Clearly, the success of almost any large program is dependent on effective leadership. Writing about one-to-one iPad programs, Salerno and Vonhof (2011) wrote, "Successful schools will have a senior administrative leader driving this initiative. . . . [He or she] must be a champion for technology and have sufficient knowledge to coordinate an internal and external technological vision." The leaders must then share the vision with all key stakeholders. School board members, administrators, teachers, and parents must all be informed and have a good understanding of the project.

Then representatives from each group should be chosen to help coordinate the dissemination of information both prior to and during the initiation of the program. Monlieu Elementary School, in High Point, North Carolina, began their one-to-one initiative in the fall of 2011. Prior to the fall, an excellent program guide, titled "1 to 1 EmPoweredLearning Initiative, 2011–2012 Policy, Procedures, and Information Guide," was developed that offered clear explanations of how the school would be handling the distribution and care of nearly 500 iPads. On the whole, this is an excellent guide covering an iPad one-to-one initiative (1 to 1 EmPoweredLearning, 2011).

The second critical area to address is *assuring system setup*, which includes arranging for a professionally installed, wireless network with adequate bandwidth. Without that, screams of frustration may be heard throughout the school as an inadequate Wi-Fi network slows to a mere snail's pace.

Schools and districts must assure that their networks, bandwidth, and servers are all able to handle the significant increase in technology use. No educator wants to stymie the learning simply because of improper preparations in this area. A second router might be considered to avoid outages. Qualified technicians should be involved throughout the planning process to assure success of the initiative.

Arranging for security and maintenance is another very critical area. Without adequate planning for both the security and maintenance of the devices, excitement over a new iPad initiative could quickly turn to disaster. Security involves the question of ownership. For the majority of universities and private schools, the students become the owners of the iPads and therefore must assume the responsibility for security and maintenance of their devices. However, the majority of public schools opt to retain possession and thereby assume primary responsibility for the iPads.

By owning the iPads, the schools have far greater control over the use of the devices, including the prevention of inappropriate material. In response to the growing number of mobile devices that are used in schools and business alike, various software packages have been developed to manage and support large numbers of devices.

Remote access of devices is also possible. Apple does provide some built-in functionality that allows for monitoring its devices. Additionally, insurance should always be acquired to cover theft and damages to the devices. An article titled "The Importance of iPad Insurance in an Educational Setting" offers a good starting point with a list of four providers (Walsh, 2012).

The fourth critical area, *providing ongoing training*, may appear obvious, but it is frequently shortchanged. Ample training needs to be provided for the administrators and faculty well before the students receive their devices. Teachers need adequate time to explore and become comfortable with a collection of apps. The devices should be distributed to faculty at least six to eight months prior to the beginning of the initiative. Professional development sessions should be offered as soon as the teachers receive their iPads. Finally, as a new school year begins, training sessions should be available every month or two during the school year.

Earlier, parents were mentioned as being among the key stakeholders in any one-to-one initiative. As such, they should not be overlooked when sharing information and training about the iPads. Parents may fail to understand the value of the devices and become frustrated with seeing their child absorbed by yet another technology device. Training in the use of the device should be optional for parents, but it remains critical to schedule ample informational meetings.

The fifth area of the keys for success brings to mind a famous quote made by Everett Dirksen: "I am a man of fixed and unbending principles, the first of which is to be flexible at all times" (Ashworth, 2001, p. 11). *Welcoming flexibility* is essential for the success of any iPad initiative. Even with an immense amount of time invested in planning, some things will inevitably go wrong. An inability to be flexible with certain aspects of a new program can almost assure failure.

Two very exciting benefits of the one-to-one classroom deserve to be recognized here. First, the one-to-one iPad initiative is the only method for using iPads that allows for a truly paperless classroom. Second, perhaps the most exciting aspect of the iPad is how easily it facilitates a *flipped classroom*. The flipped classroom, also known as the inverted classroom, is an instructional strategy that has been recognized for its ability to allow teachers to transform the classroom by primarily serving as the "guide on the side" rather than as the "sage on the stage." The paperless classroom is a direct benefit of flipping the classroom.

The basic strategy for the flipped classroom is that each lesson is initiated outside the classroom with each student working independently. Using the iPad, teachers can create their own presentations for the students to watch at home with apps such as Educreations or Prezi. Discussions can be initiated through Edmodo. Assessments can be made through Socrative.

Assignments could be submitted through Dropbox or Evernote. Those apps will all be explained in detail later. The students then come to class equipped with a basic knowledge about the new topic. The ultimate goal of flipping the class is to then allow the teacher to spend quality time in the classroom going into more depth on each topic and assisting students as they gain greater understanding.

The issue of students' ability to access the Internet at home has been raised. In a recent report titled the Digest of Education Statistics (2011), researchers found that 85.2 percent of persons age 3 years and older were using the Internet. From that group 89.1 percent were using the Internet at home.

Although those percentages have been increasing in recent years, the students who do not have Internet access at home should not be ignored.

Providing a DVD with the needed videos would be able to take care of many of those students. Others could be encouraged to stay for after-school sessions or to go to a nearby library where Internet access would be available.

As mentioned above, the second benefit of one-to-one iPad initiatives is the ability to achieve a paperless classroom. In the typical classrooms of the past, students were coming to class with homework in hand. Unable to immediately access student understanding from that homework, teachers were usually forging ahead with new topics, thus magnifying any existing misunderstandings. However, with the flipped classroom, no papers are brought to class; rather the teacher initiates class by clarifying any confusion that the students shared the previous night through their work with the various apps.

For the remaining class time, students work independently or in groups to delve more deeply into the topic. Both the work at home and in the classroom is done entirely on the iPad. As the students leave the classroom, they are ready to move onto the next assigned topic. No papers have exchanged hands.

At the end of a yearlong study at a university in Texas, the researcher concluded, "The paperless classroom is a reality for both the instructor and student. I see the iPad and its educational applications as critical in the development of mobile learning" (Shepherd & Reeves, 2011). A one-to-one initiative is the only way for iPads to be used to their fullest potential.

Classroom Set of iPads

As mentioned above, the one-to-one scenario is the ideal but may not always be feasible. The failure to initiate a one-to-one program usually relates to being unable to acquire either adequate funds or adequate support. Many schools settle on purchasing a limited number of classroom sets of iPads. Those sets may be located in the classrooms of designated teachers, or they may be located in a central location to be checked out as needed.

Administrators may believe that having some classroom sets will be a good way to test whether a one-to-one initiative would be valuable and feasible to initiate at a later time. However, educators should be aware that some of the activities that run smoothly with one-to-one programs may not be possible with just a classroom set. The capabilities of iPads are simply not the same in those two scenarios. The way that teachers use them and the way that they approach them needs to be vastly different. In short, the iPad is not designed to be shared (Salerno & Vonhof, 2011).

Since iPads were designed to be used only by single users, the shared scenario can lead to a collection of frustrations. First, it is important to realize that every time a student saves something to a community iPad, the next user of the iPad will have access to whatever has been saved. Thus, the saved item can be changed, copied, or even deleted by an irresponsible or careless second user. Some have suggested that students should just email an assignment to the teacher and then delete it from the iPad. Emails can be sent from an iPad, but attaching a file is not possible.

Some apps do allow you to email a file directly from within the app. However, every user of a specific iPad will be emailing through the same email account. Each iPad can be associated with only a single email account. That builds in some dangers, as anyone that picks up that iPad could send anything they want to anybody. There are some safe ways for transmitting assignments, but each app usually requires different techniques.

Regardless of the activity, teachers need to have very strict guidelines when using classroom sets. Throughout a semester or year, students should always be assigned a specific iPad to give teachers the ability to track potential problems. Class rules should limit the amount of movement around the classroom, and touching iPads that are not your own should be forbidden. Other guidelines should include having clean hands and not bringing food or drink to class. Students need to understand that their teacher always expects and strongly enforces rules for showing nothing but the respectful use of the iPads.

A professor who works in the Department of Computer and Information Technology at Lipscomb University once commented, "Managing a cart of iPads is not trivial." Several companies sell carts designed to store, sync, and recharge iPads. In addition, an Internet search for "build your own iPad cart" will provide several other options.

Managing a cart takes technical support. In addition, someone always needs to be responsible for routinely taking the iPads through the processes of both syncing and recharging. At the end of the syncing process, the iPads will need to be disconnected from the computer so that the recharging process can be initiated. Special care should always be taken with charging, syncing, and protecting the devices (Dunn, 2012). Directions for those tasks are provided with whichever cart a school has decided to purchase.

Several years of experience has shown that rolling carts work best when assigned to a designated teacher rather than being available to be checked out by any classroom teacher:

> Carts that rotate through several classrooms force teachers to take time away from learning, create a nightmare of student accounts, and often focus attention on workflow systems rather than learning. . . . Instead schools should be allocating them to a few select pilot classrooms for an entire year. (Daccord, 2012).

Teachers who use iPads should fully recognize the power of these devices and be willing to spend the extra time to set them up properly before students have access to them. Before being allowed to open the first app, students should understand the classroom guidelines for using the device. They should stay focused on specific classroom activities and avoid gravitating to the Internet or other distracting apps that are outside the day's assignments.

With a few careful steps, teachers can assure that students are engaged and learning is achieved. One of the best strategies to use with a set of iPads would be discovery learning. That inquiry-based strategy requires that students take ownership of their own learning. A multitude of apps lend themselves well to this strategy.

Small Number of iPads
With only a small number of iPads, teachers can use them for group work or for competitive teams. Almost any lesson plan that incorporates small groups could be enhanced with the use of iPads. One third-grade teacher from Nebraska wrote, "The key to getting results from just a few iPads is to create a classroom structure where the teacher can meet with each student in a small group setting every day" (Abeling, 2012).

In short, the teacher needs to rotate while the students are engaged. Having just a few iPads can be effective not only at the elementary level but even at the university level. Tracy Futhey, chief information officer at Duke University, commented that when Duke "purchased a handful as loaners for faculty, the wait list grew to six weeks overnight" (della Cava, 2010).

Having a small number of iPads works very smoothly for lessons that use cooperative learning. With cooperative learning, students are set off into groups, working collaboratively on assigned projects. In a history class, for example, groups could be assigned to study various aspects of a specific time period. From an article on ESL learning: "[T]he iPad naturally lends itself to cooperative learning. The students can break into pairs or groups. . . . This greatly enhances their ability to learn" (Stevens, 2011). In later chapters, cooperative learning will be referenced several times as lessons are provided for using specific apps in specific subject areas.

The iPad as a Single Device in the Classroom
With the projection system set up, a teacher could have apps running that would allow groups of students to participate as teams, perhaps for classroom competitions. Other options for using a single iPad in the classroom include using the document camera or having a workstation with a designated iPad.

One elementary teacher polled her colleagues to learn how they used their own personal iPads in the classroom: 7 percent projected to a screen, 15 percent used a doc camera, 15 percent "gather[ed] around on a carpet or in a large group," 23 percent passed it around, and 9 percent used unspecified other methods (Brown, 2012). If a projection system is unavailable, the document camera is a viable option.

Tips for the One iPad Classroom (Butkus, 2012) website offers suggestions for sharing iPads in the elementary classroom. Specifically, the author of this blog describes fourteen different techniques for using a single iPad with young children. Those strategies include methods for differentiating instruction, taking quizzes, and improving reading.

The site also includes links to posters that are available showing classroom rules for using the iPad. Next to a picture of small hourglasses, the blog suggests that students could be allowed to use the iPad only until the sand ran through the hourglass. However, the teacher could also use a variety of apps as timers, including a basic alarm app.

Research shows that learning is strongly enhanced by having students actively engaged in their own learning. Teachers of all grade levels can effectively use academic games as one of the techniques for engaging their students with a single iPad. This strategy is particularly useful for review sessions on days prior to testing and can be used at all grade levels. Mistakes that students make can show teachers the areas that might need to be further addressed.

The iPad App Store is replete with apps that could stimulate learning in the classroom through the use of a game on a single iPad. For example, a middle school or high school geography teacher could use the TapQuiz Maps app. This app allows the teacher to pick one of thirty-two areas of the world. For the game, the class could be divided into groups of five. Of course, teachers can adjust the specific rules to best fit their classroom needs; in one scenario, a representative from each group might be asked to go first.

When the teacher hands the iPad to the first group, the first student starts the game. The names of countries appear at the top of the screen, and that student would be expected to tap the correct country. The score for the first student is recorded as his or her team's score. Then the iPad is handed to other groups. As the iPad makes its second round, different students play. The timer on this game continues to run until all countries are picked correctly, so the teacher might want to have a time limit for each student. This is just one of a myriad of apps that can be used for games with a single iPad.

Reflections on Chapter 1

This chapter has given a succinct overview of exactly what an iPad is, why it should be used, and some examples of how the device could be used. In short, the iPad is not just another computer but rather a device that has unique capabilities for engaging students and enhancing learning. The iPad can most effectively be used in classrooms where each student is using his or her own iPad. However, with some adjustments, the devices can also effectively be used in other classrooms that have classroom sets, a small number of devices, or even a single iPad.

Although research has shown that having a single owner will allow the iPad to most easily facilitate learning, the device still remains versatile. In one classroom, the iPad can serve as a tool for individual students. Then, in the next classroom, a teacher may be using it for a whole-class presentation. On other days, iPads can be used with either small groups or a full classroom of students.

Within schools, whichever scenario is being played out, adequate training for the involved educators is crucial. Administrators and teachers alike need to understand the hardware, as well as the software. The iPad is not just a toy. It's an educator's tool that is well worth the investment in cost and time.

CHAPTER TWO

—◦◦◦—

Apps and Techniques
for All Subject Areas

Introduction

Apps are the power behind the iPad. As mentioned in chapter 1, iPads cannot perform as they were intended without having apps. Using an iPad without apps would be like buying an 84-inch flat-screen television, bringing it home, and using it for watching only DVDs. Without access to a signal, a television has limited usefulness and certainly cannot function as it was intended. Similarly, without apps, iPads cannot function as they were intended.

Apps breathe life into an iPad. Apps are the software for this unique device. Because of the importance of apps, the majority of this book, as well as that of the companion book, focuses on those delightful inventions and specifically on educational apps. Starting with chapter 4, each chapter focuses on a selection of apps for a specific subject.

However, do not go there just yet! Take heed to the warning recently given by educator Tom Daccord (2012): "The most common mistake teachers make with iPads is focusing on subject-specific apps. In doing so, many completely overlook the full range of possibilities with the iPad." This chapter, as well as the next chapter, begins an amazing venture into learning about the potential of apps that can be used across all subject areas.

Simply doing a search on the Internet for the most powerful educational apps usually brings up lists of top 10, top 20, and so forth. This book could have included a generated list of lists. Alas, there are already too many such annoying creations in education. However, attempting to select the current top apps, at any point in time, can set one's mind in a spiraling journey. The problem remains that many educators struggled with just how to swim skillfully through the immensity of the app pool.

Based on extensive readings, many personal interviews, and several years of personal experience, the selection for this book of an elite few became almost obvious. Chapter 2 has a description of nine apps, covering five major areas:

1. Built-in camera and photos apps (along with Text on Photo app)
2. A presentation app (Prezi)
3. A note-taking app (Evernote)
4. A file-sharing app (Dropbox)
5. Social learning platform apps for teachers (Edmodo and Schoology)

Chapter 3 continues with fifteen more unique and valuable apps. The apps in chapters 2 and 3 should be considered essential to any twenty-first-century classroom. The apps in this chapter come up time and time again as being on most highly rated lists. Because of the value of these nine apps, descriptions that are longer than any of those for the other apps in this book are provided. Do not underestimate the value of these apps!

Built-In Camera and Photo Apps

On March 7, 2012, the announcement of the iPad 3 brought a great deal of fanfare. Within hours, news sites and blogs were sending out reports of the changes in the snapshot and video capabilities of the new iPad. One site explained: "The newest device release from the tech giant marks the third-generation of its category defining mobile device, featuring a new Retina display, Apple's new A5X chip with quad-core graphics and a 5 megapixel iSight camera with advanced optics for capturing photos and 1080p HD video" (Ciardiello, 2012). In short, far better graphics and videos were now possible!

Those advancements allow teachers to create more engaging presentations and to assign more stimulating assignments for students by including quality images. In less than a year, more fanfare came on October 23, 2012, with the announcement of the iPad 4 and the mini-iPad. The iPad 4 has an A6X chip and a processor with nearly twice the speed. Apple is always looking for ways to improve the quality of this device. This chapter includes an introduction to only a few camera and photo apps and how to use them. In several other areas of this two-book set, there will be other descriptions of ways to enhance features of a variety of apps.

⟊⟊⟊

Built-In Camera App
Apple, Inc.
Cost: Free—included with purchase of iPad

The Camera app is something that every teacher should be using to personalize his or her teaching. Teachers could highlight their students' work on class websites. Then each student's work could have a picture associated with it that shows the student who created the assignment. Directions for using the camera are very straightforward. To start, simply tap on the camera icon, which immediately opens the camera lens, through the backward-aiming camera.

Users may hold the iPad in a horizontal or vertical alignment, but they should be careful to keep their fingers away from the camera lens. The best orientation, for most pictures, is to hold the iPad horizontally, with any cover hanging down. The rear camera is then on the top left. A picture is taken by tapping on the camera graphic, which is always positioned halfway up the right side.

If users want to use the forward-facing camera, they should look at the bottom menu, where there is a little camera with two curved arrows, as shown in Figure 2.1. That is a toggle switch between the rear-facing and forward-facing cameras. The screen always shows which camera is active. The rear-facing camera is of a higher quality than the forward-facing camera and is the camera that is used most often.

After deciding on which camera to use, users need to decide whether to make a still picture or a video. Again, there is a toggle switch that is just to the right of the camera switch. Drag the button to the right for video and keep it at the left for a still picture. Note that there is also an Options button to the lower left that allows users to add grid lines for more carefully framing still pictures.

A recording of a shutter click is heard whenever a snapshot is taken. The newly taken image can be viewed by tapping on the thumbnail image of the picture that resides in the lower left corner of the screen. That will take the

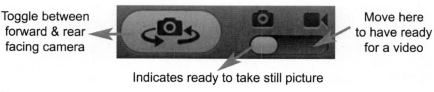

Toggle between forward & rear facing camera

Move here to have ready for a video

Indicates ready to take still picture

Figure 2.1. Camera app

viewer to the Photos area of the iPad. To return to the Camera app for more picture taking, users should tap on the blue Done button on the top right.

Using the video app is just as easy. Users toggle on the lower right icon, as shown in Figure 2.1, to activate the video camera. The circular icon that is shown with still pictures changes from a graphic of a camera to a circle with a red button in the center. Users tap the button to start recording. While a camera is recording, the red center is always flashing. To stop the recording, users tap the button again. Just like with still pictures, users tap the small icon in the lower left of the screen to view the video.

The ability to take a quick screen shot of the iPad screen becomes invaluable for handouts with iPad instructions. Users do not need the Camera app to take a screen shot of what is showing on the users' iPads. All they need to do is to briefly tap on the on–off button, which is at the top right of the iPad when held vertically and, *at the same time*, tap on the home button. After the shutter click, users can view the image from the thumbnail, at the lower left, or from the Photos app, which is described below.

—✦✦✦—

Photos App
Apple, Inc.
Cost: Free—included with purchase of iPad

Every new iPad comes with the Photos app already preinstalled. By default, the app is assigned a location on the dock at the base of the home screen, although it can be moved to any location users wish. All screen shots, pictures, and videos that are taken with the iPad reside in Photos. On the opening screen, the top menu shows the following categories: Photos, Photo Stream, Albums, and Places. Each of those areas has a unique function.

The Photos tab shows all the users' photos—the good, the bad, and the ugly—in chronological order. Users can delete the ugly by tapping on the thumbnail to make the photo full screen. Then users just tap on the trash can, on the upper menu bar. A red Delete button appears to confirm the intent to delete. Users can delete a group of images by tapping on the Edit button at the top right, then tapping on all the unwanted images. A check mark appears on the selected ones, and then tapping on the Delete button, on the top left, can finish the process. Anytime that a menu bar disappears, users can tap in the area where the menu bar had been, and it will reappear.

When users open a single picture, they can tap on the Edit button, at the top, to bring up a selection of tools on a menu bar, at the bottom of the picture: Rotate, Enhance, Red-Eye, and Crop. The magic wand automatically enhances images. If the enhancements look good, users should tap on the yellow Save button. For removing red eyes, users can tap on the Red-Eye button and then zoom in close to each eye. Users can tap on each eye to adjust the color and then tap on the Apply button to view the image of the person with the red eyes removed.

Still within the main Photos tab, users can tap on the Slideshow button, at the top right, to select some music. Then a streaming slideshow of all the images and videos begins. However, most users want to sort their pictures before initiating a slideshow. Directions to do that is covered in the Album section.

The Photo Stream area may seem confusing at first. Just like the Photo area, Photo Stream is a place where all the screen shots, images, and videos reside. However, the Photo Stream has a direct link to the iCloud. As long as an iCloud account has been set up and the Photo Stream setting has been turned on in the Settings area of the iPad, then every image and video that is taken on any of the users' iOS devices will automatically be copied to the Photo Stream area.

That synchronization process normally makes the Photo Stream area much larger than that of the Photos area. This functionality is a wonderful feature of the iPad. On a recent Apple blog, a writer suggested that the Photo Stream could be thought of as "a replacement for a camera's memory card" (Wakefield, 2011). The Photo Stream can hold up to a one thousand pictures from the past thirty days and automatically recycles after that to make more room.

The Album is an area that allows pictures to be grouped. To start working there, users tap on the Album tab and then tap on Edit on the top right menu. Next, they tap on the + button on the top left of the menu, which allows them to name a new album. After tapping on the Save button, all images from the Photos section appear. Tap on a photo that is intended for the newly created album, and a check mark appears on the picture. After selecting all of the desired images, users should click the Done button, on the top right menu bar. That is how to organize images and have them ready for the Slideshow.

To begin the slideshow, users tap on the album to open it and then tap on the Slideshow button. Again, the option to add music is available. This is a great way for teachers to review class trips or any classroom activity either for students or for those school parents' nights. To determine the speed of a slideshow, users can make adjustments in the Settings area. On the left side, they select Photos & Camera. Options are available for setting the timing to two, three, five, ten, or twenty seconds. There are also options to Repeat or Shuffle.

The last major area of the Photos app is titled Places. A map there has a red pushpin marking every area where the iPad has been used to take a picture. Tapping on a specific pin shows a user all of the images taken in that location. The Slideshow is also available in this area. This is the quick and easy way to see a slideshow of sites visited.

⸺✺⸺

Text on Photo
handyCloset, Inc.
Cost: $ 0.99

Text on Photo is one of many apps for creatively writing text on Photos. The text can add a very professional appearance, and it is easy to use for both teachers and students.

When users open the app, they first click on the word "Photo," on the top menu bar. That brings up a drop-down menu, showing the iPad's Camera Roll, Albums, and Photo Stream so that any picture can easily be selected. Once the picture is selected, users should tap on the word "Text" on the top menu, which brings up a window for typing the text.

After users tap on the Done button, a menu at the bottom provides an array of fonts, colors, and styles to play with, as shown in Figure 2.2. The box around the text is there merely to allow users to resize or rotate the text. Each corner of the box has a unique function. The top row of colors is for the text border color, and the second row is for the text color itself. At any point, an image can be saved to the camera roll, but tapping on the text allows for further adjustments. The image in Figure 2.2 is the result of using white font with a colored border. The new creations are saved to the Camera Roll without replacing the original photo.

There are innumerable possibilities for the classroom uses of this app. Images could be part of a slideshow in a history class. Students could also be given images as part of a WebQuest and then be asked to label them appropriately. A collection of images from field trips could be assigned to groups of students, who would then be responsible for labeling the pictures. And, of course, a collection of annotated images could be displayed at a parents' night.

Presentation Apps

The apps listed in this section are more than just tools for those teachers who are still hooked on using direct instruction. Educreations is designed to create short video clips, which can be shared directly with students or inserted

Figure 2.2.   Text on Photo tools

into other apps. Prezi is more like users' presentations on steroids. Nearpod, another free, high quality presentation app has been gaining considerable popularity in school recently. Only Educreations and Prezi are discussed here but users are encouraged to check out the websites below. With all three of these apps, let the creative juices flow!

Websites related to Nearpod:

- Designer's article: www.nearpod.com/school/;
- Interview with founder: edtechdigest.wordpress.com/2012/05/10/inter view-getting-cozy-with-nearpod/;
- The Journal article (October, 2012): thejournal.com/articles/2012/10/ 09/slide-sharing-ipad-app-nearpod-like-powepoint-on-steroids.aspx ?utm_source=twitterfeed&utm_medium=twitter

—⁓—

Educreations Interactive Whiteboard
Educreations, Inc.
Website: www.educreations.com/
Cost: Free

Educreations is far more than just a plain whiteboard. It is a *recordable* whiteboard! Users can insert text and/or graphics, then record directions, and finally save a short video file. Being able to create such a file makes this app perfect for the flipped classroom. Educreations is fully functional either through the web or the iPad app. One very important fact to remember about Educreations is that, unlike many iPad apps, *Educreations does NOT automatically save work.* Even clicking on the Done button on the home screen does not save work. Only by using the red "rec," or record, button can work be saved.

So, users should always plan ahead to record succinct and clear messages while writing on the screen. The top menu bar, shown in Figure 2.3, is very intuitive, with the selection of four colors allowed for either finger drawing or typing of text. However, by giving a second tap to any of those four colors, users are provided with a selection of ten colors. The large "T" inserts a textbox. Tapping and holding on the lower-right corner of an inserted textbox resizes it.

Tapping on the graphic icon brings a drop-down menu, showing the four areas where images can be found: Camera, Photos, Dropbox, and Web. Tapping on Camera opens up the iPad camera for a still shot with either the forward- or rear-facing camera. A preview of the image is then shown; two buttons on the bottom menu allow for a Retake or a save by tapping on the Use button. If users select the Use button, a menu at the bottom of the image allows them to delete, rotate, duplicate, fit height or width, and lock. If that menu disappears, users can bring it up again by tapping and holding anywhere on the image.

Figure 2.3. Top menu bar for Educreations

From the drop-down menu mentioned in the previous paragraph, users can search for images in the Photos area of the iPad or in Dropbox. Clicking on the web opens up a Google Images page. The blue hand, to the left of the text icon in Figure 2.3, is activated anytime a picture is inserted. A one-finger tap, hold, and drag allows the images to be moved. A two-finger pinch resizes an image. That is, users place two fingers on the iPad and bring them closer together to decrease the size of the image and spread fingers apart to increase the image size.

Also, the ever-valuable undo and redo icons are located on the top menu, followed by the "X," which serves as a delete button. Tapping on the little square icon on the bottom left menu with the folded corner brings up a pop-up menu with four selections for the background: white paper, lined paper, graph paper, or coordinate grid—a great option for math teachers.

When users are ready to record, they should tap on the Rec button. After the recording, users should tap the Done button and then select either Save or Start Over. If users select Save, they are then asked to type in a title and description. Also they can select Private or Public.

Next, a selection of a subject area is requested, although that can be skipped by selecting Other. Finally, a window comes up to Create an Account or Sign in. Editing previously created files is not possible with Educreations. The best users can do is to delete the file by tapping on the trash can and starting over. What is the moral of the story? Plan ahead and abandon any underlying thoughts of perfection. The benefits far outweigh this one disadvantage.

Also, as a final thought, please know that there are a couple of other apps that offer similar features to Educreations: ShowMe and ScreenChomp. I prefer Educreations for several reasons, but the last site in the list below provides more specifics about each of the three.

Sampling of Websites with Educreations Information, Tutorials, or Samples
- Educreations website, which allows Support and Feedback from the tab on the left side of the window: www.educreations.com/
- iTunes Preview: itunes.apple.com/us/app/educreations-interactive -whiteboard/id478617061?ls=1&mt=8
- Tutorial for using on iPad (example for middle school math or science class): www.youtube.com/watch?v=gYcdhaPr7G8&feature=related
- Tutorial for using online features: www.youtube.com/watch?v=dU -Gcer-5Ig
- iPads in kindergarten: ipadsink.blogspot.com/2012/08/educreations -writing-lesson.html

- Educreations with fourth-grade classroom: shutthedoorandteach.blog spot.com/2013/04/learning-to-use-educreations-on-ipad.html
- Viewpoint and samples from seventh-grade math teacher: mistergoode .blogspot.com/2012/06/educreations.html
- High school physics class: www.pasadenaisd.org/it/spotlight/SOHO_ Educreations/default.htm
- Differences between Screen Chomp, Show me, and Educreations: www .educreations.com/lesson/view/differences-between-screen-chomp -show-me-educreati/2400258/

———∿———

Prezi
Prezi, Inc.
Website: prezi.com/ipad
Cost: Free
PowerPoint has been such a standard for so long that when Prezi was new many teachers resisted the change to the whole new approach to presentations. Gradually, Prezi is being used more routinely. Many now realize that Prezi is far more engaging than any other presentation software to date. A professor and archivist at Yale University commented:

> Prezi allows users to create live relationships between blocks of text or thought bubbles, dynamically—and daresay entertainingly—linking both pieces of information and the concepts that connect them. A recent classroom experience solidified my love for Prezi. . . . The difference this made in this research education session was dramatic. Prezi is visually stunning, and it engaged the students and focused their attention. (Pinto, 2011)

Whenever students are engaged and focused, learning becomes the natural by-product. Teachers often ponder about how they can garner the attention of their students. Prezi is an effective tool for addressing that need. With the original two iPads, the presentations could not be created on the iPad, only viewed. However, in recent years, Prezi has added an increasing number of features that allow for existing presentations to be edited and new presentations to be created. Whether on the web or on an iPad, an account with Prezi must be set up before using this app.

The following directions here are purely for working with Prezi on the iPad. Users start creating a new Prezi by tapping on the blue New Prezi button, on the top right. The new Prezi will immediately have a default background, with five frames ready to have information added. Users can tap on the wrench, on the top menu bar, to bring up a selection of other templates.

An assortment of templates is provided, each with several frames that can be moved or deleted later.

New frames can be added by tapping on the blue Add Frame button. In Figure 2.4, the last frame is selected on the left menu. The Prezi viewer then zooms to show a close-up of the frame, which has two subframes, all ready to be filled with text. Also, in the lower menu are several options for changing the layout of a frame. After adding the text, users can save the Prezi by tapping on the home icon, on the top menu bar. Existing presentations can be edited with a text and camera menu, on the right side of the screen.

Working on presentations from a computer remains a bit easier. However, it has been exciting to see that the designer has slowly been adding features to the app so that adaptations have been getting progressively easier. Stay tuned. More features are undoubtedly in the works! And, in the meantime, check out the following sites for additional information.

Sampling of Websites with Prezi Information
- Prezi viewer iPad app manual: prezi.com/learn/ipad-support/
- Prezi for iPad, the reality: ipadcto.com/2011/01/12/prezi-for-ipad-brings -non-linear-presentations-to-ipad/

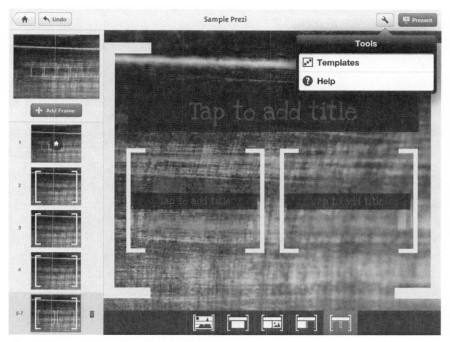

Figure 2.4.   New Prezi with default settings

Note Taking

Evernote
Evernote Corporation
Website: evernote.com
Cost: Free; $4.99/month or $44.99/year for premium; also available on Android

    The title of "Note Taking" really sells short the power and capabilities of Evernote. Possibly a more appropriate title would be "Tool for Remembering and Organizing Everything." In the often chaotic and multitasking life of a teacher, this app can offer calm and a smooth path to being in control and organized. Doesn't that sound glorious? The features of Evernote are straightforward and easy to apply.

    At the top of the website page for Evernote, their tag line is "Remember Everything." That is exactly what the app can do! It "remembers" notes, bookmarks, audio files, video files, pictures, and more. Whatever users wants to save can be saved and organized in notebooks. Any ideas can be jotted down. Also, sparks of genius can easily be saved in audio files. Another spectacular feature of Evernote is that it can be created either on the web or on users' iPads, and it is automatically synced with other devices every time something is added.

    On the iPad, users do not need an Internet connection to work on this app, although a connection is obviously needed for work to be synced with other devices. A few features in Evernote work only on the website.

    In November 2012, Evernote took on a whole new appearance for iPad users with the introduction of Version 5. Previously the appearance was nearly the same as it appeared on the web. Now, the appearance is as shown in Figure 2.5. Developers wrote that the driving force behind the redesign was "to make all major functions accessible within two taps" (Sinkov, 2012). Signing up can be done either on the website or from an iPad. The directions here are solely for using Evernote on the iPad. However, several tutorials for using it on the web are available on the web and can be found with a quick Google search.

    On the iPad, users' Evernote user names always appear in the upper-left corner of the app's home screen. The three icons below the users' names are labeled in Figure 2.5. The top icon allows a new note to be added. That note can be dictated by simply tapping on the microphone key on the pop-up keyboard, which is just to the left of the spacebar. Otherwise, users can type a note. Pasting in copied text or URLs is also easy. When typing a note, the top menu provides the following six choices:

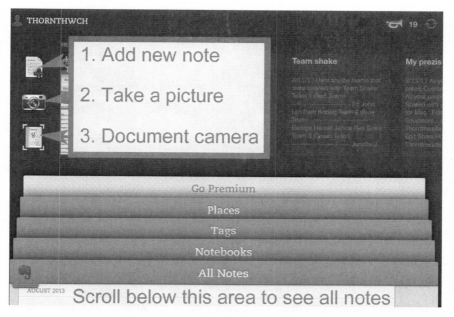

THORNTHWCH   19

1. Add new note

2. Take a picture

3. Document camera

Team shake   My prezis

Go Premium

Places

Tags

Notebooks

All Notes

AUGUST 2013 Scroll below this area to see all notes

Figure 2.5.   **Evernote home screen, with additional labels added**

1. The Camera allows users to take pictures. When finished taking pictures, users tap the check mark at the lower right. The first time users use this feature, a window pops up asking their permission to access the Camera Roll. That allows the pictures to be saved both to the note and to the Camera Roll. Users can then see the pictures embedded in their notes. Text can be added either above or below the images. When finished with the note, users tap the Close button in the upper-left corner.

2. The second icon on the top menu brings up users' Camera Roll. By tapping on any of the pictures there, they are able to insert them into a note.

3. The third icon, a little microphone, allows users to create an audio file. Users simply tap it to record, speak clearly, and then tap Done. The files can be as long as ninety minutes. Then users see the file, with the name Evernote and a number. Users may tap in the title area to assign a specific title to their notes and also to add text in the body of the notes. Then they simply close the file. Unfortunately, at the present time, the audio quality does not seem to be as good as the quality of files generated by some other audio apps that are discussed in chapter 3.

4. The trash can icon allows users to delete any selected notes.

5. The little "i" icon provides users information about the notes.
6. The magnifying glass allows users to search for any specific text within the notes.

Each note also comes with four icons on the bottom menu, from left to right:

1. The first icon allows users to trigger a notification on a specified day.
2. Logically, the star icon marks the note with a star.
3. This icon opens the note in Skitch so the note can be edited with all the Skitch tools. This app allows users to annotate images and video; the app is discussed in chapter 3.
4. The shared icon allows users to print or share via Facebook or email.

Another menu is not apparent until users start typing in the main body of the text. These selections are listed below:

- 1–4 Bold, italicize, underline, and strikethrough
- 5 The exclamation mark allows users to highlight the text.
- 6 The box with an arrow creates a hyperlink from a pop-up window.
- 7–8 The paragraph icon brings up a pop-up menu that allows users to format the text into a section, subsection, paragraph, or block quote. With the next icon, the text can be simplified or converted to plain text.
- 9 The box with a check mark inserts a checkbox at the beginning of an area that allows readers to indicate a selection. This stays active until users delete the last inserted box.
- 10–11 Clicking here creates bulleted and numbered lists.
- 12–13 The horizontal arrows allow users to tab across or back in the note area.
- 14–15 The last two icons are the standard undo and redo buttons.

Tapping the camera icon on the home screen allows users to take pictures, just as is done with the Camera app. Each time users take pictures through this app, the number of images is indicated with a number in the lower right of the screen. When users are finished with picture taking, they tap the blue check mark below the number. The images that users took are then embedded in a note, waiting to be shared. The home screen Document Camera functions similar to how the camera functions, although the quality of text is greatly enhanced when using the Document Camera.

A few frustrations currently exist with Evernote. One is the inability to control font size as users type notes. This is something that may change in the future. A second frustration, as mentioned earlier, is that the audio quality is not quite as good as making audio files with some other apps.

Up to this point, only the notes have been discussed. The beauty of Evernote is its ability to organize notes into notebooks. When users select the green Notebooks folder from the home screen, all notebooks are shown, arranged alphabetically. No matter how many notebooks users have, the top left area, enclosed with a dotted line, is always ready to be tapped for the creation of a new notebook. On the web, users can create notebooks within notebooks. Those notebooks within notebooks will show and can be used on the iPad. A white band under the name of a notebook indicates that multiple notebooks are within the one.

The elephant, at the top left of the green banner, is Evernote's logo, but on users' iPads it also serves as a link back to the home screen. Above the Notebooks green folder, shown in Figure 2.5, is a folder labeled Tags. That is where users can search for notes by the tags that they assigned to each note. It is always best to tag every note so that this alternative way for searching for notes is available.

The final green folder on the home screen is a fascinating folder labeled Places. Opening that folder reveals a map of the United States with at least two flags. One marks Redwood City, California, the home of Evernote Corporation. Tapping on that flag opens up a welcome note from Evernote. Tapping on the blue flag shows the location of the iPad where one or more notes were written. The numbers on the flags indicate how many notes were created at that location. Zooming in shows the location, down to the building level.

For those who travel, this section allows them to have some amazing documentation. For teachers, they can easily share the locations of each site. Finally, the last folder, as shown in Figure 2.5, is white, not green. Titled Go Premium, it is simply an enticement to acquire the Premium version, allowing for several more capabilities.

Those are the basics of Evernote. The advantages for personal use are obvious. However, several ideas for classroom uses are equally easy. Using the shared notebook feature is invaluable. Initially, guidelines should be provided to assist students as they set up their own accounts. They can each be required to create a notebook with specified assignments that they share with the instructor.

As users open a shared notebook, the shared icon may not be immediately visible. Users should tap and hold anywhere on the screen, and then pull down just slightly. First, the Updated/Created/Title buttons at the top allow users to sort their notes either by dates updated or created or by the titles. On the right, below the plus sign, is the familiar share icon. If users tap on that icon, a window pops up. Tapping on the Share with Individuals button allows users to add multiple email addresses, along with a message.

Other ideas for using Evernote in the classroom may become obvious as users delve more deeply into the capabilities of this app. Below is just a small sampling of ideas:

- Teachers can share notes or entire notebooks with their students. Similarly, students can share notes or entire notebooks with their teachers.
- In a flipped classroom, teachers could require students to take notes on readings done outside the classroom and then submit the notes. Questions that students have could similarly be sent to the teacher. Both those notes could be sent as text or audio files. The teacher can then address those questions at the beginning of the next day's activity, before moving on with the topic.
- Teachers could post a collection of notes and handouts from a day's class session. Those notes and handouts could be used by the students who were present to review the material. In addition, students who were absent could be expected to catch up with the work by reading that material. When the students who were absent return to school, they would then be prepared to continue along with the rest of the class. The shared notes could be in the form of snapshots of a whiteboard taken from the iPad and saved to a note.
- When teachers are absent, they can post their assignments and expectations for class activities. With those postings, students can no longer use the excuse that "the sub didn't tell us to do that."
- Students can be required to develop a professional portfolio by creating a notebook in Evernote that reflects their best material for a specific class or time period. For an English class, the portfolio could contain submitted papers. For music class, students could record and save audio files. For art class, snapshots could be taken and saved of their artwork. Even with free accounts, a snapshot could be taken of each student's work. More information on digital portfolios with Evernote is provided on the last link in the listing at the end of this section.

The descriptions above only skim the surface concerning the capabilities of this app. Below is a listing of some interesting websites that all relate to

Evernote. By searching the web further, readers can likely find even more ideas for using this app in the classroom.

Sampling of Videos and Websites with Evernote Information

- Video—Evernote at the Montclair Kimberly Academy: www.youtube .com/watch?v=60WtVZfM4dY&feature=player_embedded
- Evernote information, Version 5: itunes.apple.com/us/app/evernote/ id281796108?mt=8
- The new Evernote 5: blog.evernote.com/2012/11/08/the-new-evernote -5-for-iphone-ipad-and-ipod-touch/
- How things changed with Evernote: blog.web20classroom.org/2012/02/ how-things-changed-with-evernote.html
- Evernote as portfolio: evernotefolios.wordpress.com/category/imple- menting-evernote-in-the-classroom/
- Evernote for schools site: Resource for using Evernote in education: blog.discoveryeducation.com/blog/2012/02/17/evernote-for-schools -site-resource-for-using-evernote-in-education/
- Evernote discussion forum (excellent site to receive information on updates and to learn new tricks that others have discovered): discus- sion.evernote.com/
- 1:1 iPad initiative with Premium Evernote: www.williamstites.net/ 2010/11/11/evernote-in-the-classroom
- 10 Tips for teachers using Evernote—Education Series: blog.evernote. com/2011/01/13/10-tips-for-teachers-using-evernote-education-series/
- How to create student digital portfolios using Evernote (on the iPad): vimeo.com/42066807

File Sharing

Dropbox
Dropbox
Website: www.dropbox.com
Cost: Free for 2–18 GB; $99.99 for upgrade to Pro 100, allowing 100 GB/ year; also available on Android

As previously mentioned, Dropbox and Evernote seem to be the current most valuable apps for educators. If users search on Google for the top apps for the classroom, they will find these two apps on almost every list. Quite simply, Dropbox is a place to save all users' files, including word processing documents, PowerPoint presentations, pdf files, audio files, and video files. As with Evernote, specific folders can be shared.

The beauty of Dropbox comes from its ability to synchronize with all of users' computers and mobile devices. For example, once a file is saved on user's computers at school, almost instantaneously it is also available from their iPads. Then, when they arrive home that afternoon and open their computers, the file is waiting. No longer do users need to be frustrated that the iPad does not have a flash drive for saving files. Dropbox allows for the transfer of documents with an even easier method than using a flash drive.

Most educators and other professionals who work with a large number of files prefer Dropbox over flash drives, CDs, or any other device. Of course, a secondary location should always be used because no one should ever save an item to just one location. With Dropbox, users can also sort files into folders and then share folders with others. This allows for collaboration with colleagues. Similarly, folders can be set up for students to submit assignments.

Using Dropbox is quite simple. Creating an account is probably most easily done on the web, from the website shown by the company's icon above. Users simply provide a first and last name, an email address, and a password, and then check to agree to the terms of service. Users' email addresses serve as their user names for logging in. More information about setting up an account for syncing across all users' devices is available from the first website listed at the end of this section.

Another beautiful aspect of Dropbox is that it is free for at least 2 GB. That may not be sufficient for some educators, especially for saving a lot of graphics, audio, and video files. However, there is a way to have a free account with up to 18 GB! Dropbox adds 500 MB of free storage to users' accounts, up to 18 GB, every time they recommend the utility to a friend and he or she signs up. That amounts to approximately thirty-seven friends.

For teachers who require that students sign up for Dropbox, the 18 GB should be easy to attain. teachers can send invitations to students by using the third website listed at the end of this section. Additionally, Dropbox offers other methods for adding space, such as connecting to users' Twitter or Facebook accounts. If users still want even more space, Pro accounts start at $9.99 per month for 100 GB. However, free accounts can go a long way.

As with the other apps in this book, the directions here are primarily for using Dropbox on the iPad. After users have signed up for their accounts on the web, they can download the app on the iPad from the App Store. Users should read any Getting Started or iPad Intro pdf files, but they can easily be deleted later. Figure 2.6 shows part of a list of folders and files from the author's Dropbox, as seen on the left of the app's home screen.

The two folders at the top are folders for various classes that I have shared with students. The Grant folder was one that was shared by a colleague. Both

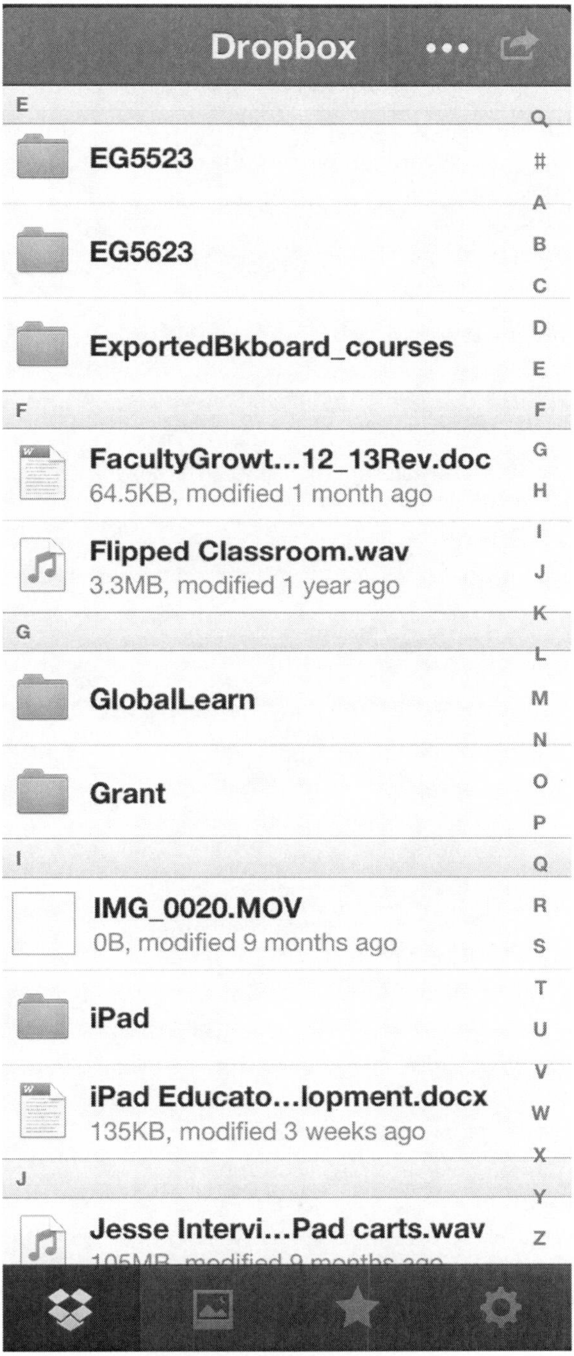

Figure 2.6. List of files and folders

a video and audio files are also on the list. The two other folders (Global-Learn and iPad) are folders created to hold a collection of related documents.

After setting up their accounts, users can begin saving files to their Drop-box. It is as simple as selecting Save as and then locating the Dropbox's location. Once installed, accessing Dropbox on a computer is as simple as clicking on the little Dropbox icon that is conveniently located on the home screen, either on the top right for a Mac or on the bottom right for a PC. The icon is snuggled there next to the time, the volume control, and other icons.

Once the files have been synchronized, users can even open Word documents on an iPad. However, the formatting may not always appear exactly the same as on a computer. Also, editing Word files on an iPad is possible but can be a bit tricky. The easiest way is to open and edit the file in Pages. More details are provided in the last link in the sampling of websites at the end of this section.

When users have a Word file open, there is a menu at the top right with three icons. The first is the share icon, which opens a drop-down menu with six selections:

1. Email
2. Text message
3. Facebook message

4. Post to Facebook
5. Tweet
6. Copy link to clipboard

The middle icon is a star, which is more important than one might think. Yes, it allows users to mark favorite files. However, in addition to bookmarking favorites, it allows users to view the files, even when offline.

For example, before taking students on a field trip to a historic site, a teacher could save a file with information about the site. Then, when at that location, the teacher could pull up the saved information and share it with the students. Other files that have not been starred are not accessible without Internet access. Dropbox keeps favorites as up to date as possible. It is always wise to tap the star for files that users might be interested in reading when outside the range of Internet access.

The star functions just like a toggle switch so users can delete the favorite designation for a file at any time by simply tapping on the star again. Tapping on the third icon on the top menu offers two options. The first option is to print the file, or the alternate selection is to Open in. This means that users can open the document in a selection of other apps, such as Pages, Evernote, or Edmodo, depending on what apps are loaded on their iPads. There is currently a limit of ten apps that are accessible this way.

Just as with the old office file cabinets that some of us still use, folders in Dropbox provide a way to group and organize the files. To create new folders, users first look at the list of their existing files and folders. They then can tap on the three dots at the top of the list and select Create Folder. In the next window, they can type in the name of the folder and then tap on the Create button. Tapping on the three dots again allows files to be uploaded.

Back on the list of files and folders, users can also select Edit from the three dots. Users select files or folders to move to the new folder and then tap on Move, at the bottom. A new window appears, which allows users to tap on the newly created folder and then tap on Choose. To delete any folders or files, users merely have to tap on the check button, at the top, select the folders or files to delete, and then tap the red delete button.

Normally, there are four icons at the bottom of the alphabetical list of the folders and files, as shown on Figure 2.6. The first is the logo of Dropbox; it provides a link back to the alphabetical list of folders and files. The second icon is the graphic of a small picture; it brings up a list of the users' graphics and video files. The third icon is a star, which brings up the files users have designated as favorites. The final icon on the list is for Settings. Note that there is a Dropbox Help link in the Settings area, which can provide valuable information for new users.

Less than half the space in this chapter has been devoted to Dropbox compared to what was written on Evernote. That does not mean that the app is less powerful. Again, both these apps are quite simply awesome! However, Dropbox is intuitive, and it does not have as broad a selection of capabilities. Also, there are many tutorials available that explain about Dropbox both on the web and on the iPad. Teachers can continue to discover new ways to apply this app, primarily through the capability of being able to save and share files.

The organization Partnership for 21st Century Skills espouses a mission to "provide tools and resources to help the U.S. education system keep up by fusing the 3Rs and 4Cs (Critical thinking and problem solving, Communication, Collaboration, and Creativity and innovation)" (2012). Communications and collaboration particularly play a major role with Dropbox. A folder can be created and shared with each one of a teacher's classes. K–12 teachers could create a folder for each subject area, with subfolders for different topics.

Collaborating with colleagues becomes a breeze when presentations and other files can be saved to a shared folder. Dropbox also allows teachers to be creative with their flipped classrooms. Handouts can be provided to students outside the classroom. Then students could be required to share a folder with their teacher for the purposes of submitting homework assignments and questions. The last site in the listing below provides other ideas from a selection of teachers who are hooked on Dropbox. Remain creative and always look for other ways to use this app!

Sampling of Videos and Websites with Dropbox Information

- Review and guide on how to use Dropbox on iPhone and iPad: www.everythingicafe.com/how-to-use-dropbox-iphone-ipad/2012/06/22/
- Automatic syncing using Dropbox: help.agilebits.com/1Password3/cloud_syncing_with_dropbox.html
- Get more free space on Dropbox: www.dropbox.com/referrals
- Dropbox for teachers: www.billselak.com/2012/dropbox
- Editing Word documents on an iPad: www.macworld.com/article/1151397/word_ipad.html

Social Learning Platforms

Edmodo
Edmodo
Website: edmodo.com
Cost: Free; also available on Android

Edmodo is reportedly "the largest, fastest growing social platform for education!" (Giacomantonio, 2012). In September 2012, exactly five years after Edmodo was founded, the site announced that it had reached the milestone of having over ten million users. Additionally, there are Edmodo users in every nation in the world! Obviously, a site with that many users must have a perceived value. This site was designed by teachers, specifically for teachers. The value for educators is immense. Through Edmodo, teachers can share content and collaborate with colleagues. In addition, they can provide discussion areas and content for their students.

Students can access homework, grades, class discussions, and notifications, as well as video and audio files. Polls and quizzes can also easily be created. In recent years, Edmodo has become so popular that there are regularly scheduled webinars, as well as an annual conference. The listing of websites for this section includes links to webinars, as well as archived sessions from the 2012 conference.

During student teaching semesters, supervisors can require prospective teachers to each set up an Edmodo account to use with his or her K–12 classes. The app allows teachers and students to have access to the site. However, as with Evernote and Dropbox, signing up for Edmodo should probably be done first on the web. The first two sites in the list at the end of this section provide instructions for doing that.

Once again, the focus here is simply on using Edmodo on the iPad. Figure 2.7 shows a snapshot of Edmodo. There are no significant differences between the web page and the iPad home screen. Apparent in the middle area of Figure 2.7 is a poll, which was answered by the thirty-one students in one university class. As soon as someone votes on that poll, the results are immediately visible. If polls are done in class, students always enjoy immediately seeing the results. Below the poll is an assignment area, where thirty-one students submitted their papers.

On the left is the main menu. The default setting is on Posts, which shows everything that was posted, with the most recent on top. The Group Management area brings up a list of folders for all the groups that users have created, as well as the groups that users may have joined. Tapping on any folder shows a list of all the members of a group.

The Progress area delineates each group, with the users and the number of items turned in by each member. Finally, the Library area provides access to all papers, web addresses, videos, and audio files.

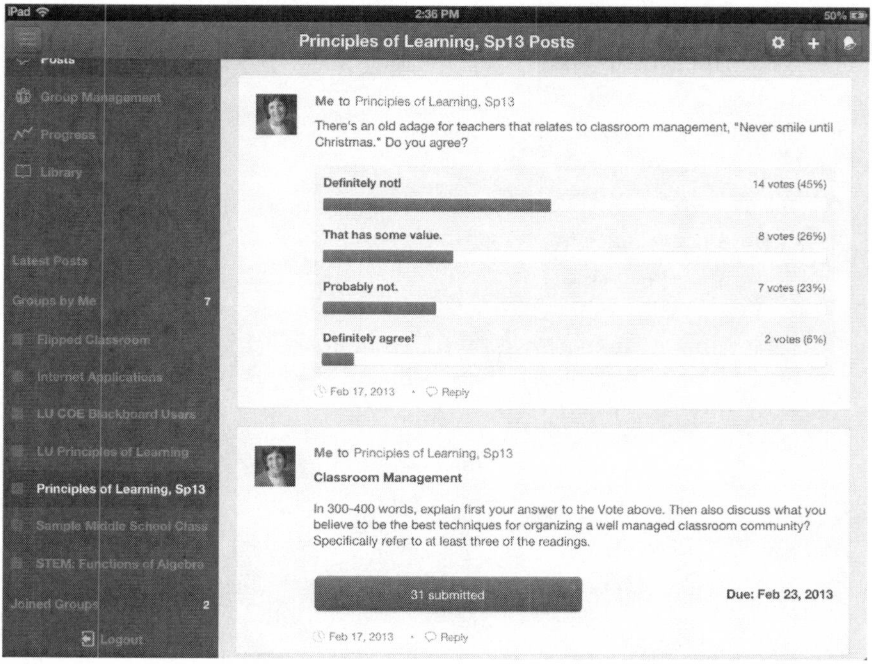

Figure 2.7. Edmodo on iPad

As with Dropbox, only minimal instruction has been provided here for Edmodo since innumerable instructive sites are available on the web. Edmodo itself has a help section, and YouTube has multiple tutorial videos. In addition, the Scottsdale Unified School District has written informative guides for both teachers and parents, which are both listed in the sampling of sites below.

Remember that parents can be allies for teachers, helping to attain classroom goals. In 2011, Edmodo added features that allowed parents to access their child's grades and assignments, without having access to the messages that the students may have sent to their teachers. Parents and teachers can communicate separately. The last website in the listing below explains about the features available to parents.

Edmodo continues to look for ways to strengthen the usefulness of this site. Recently, upgrades allowed for access to Google Docs and the iPad's Camera Roll, thus encouraging even more possibilities for collaborative work. Continue to look for newer upgrades of this app. Edmodo designers focus on the needs of teachers. This app should be on every classroom iPad.

Sampling of Videos and Websites with Edmodo Information
- How to use Edmodo in the classroom: inservice.ascd.org/technology/how-to-use-edmodo-in-the-classroom/
- Signing up for Edmodo.com (video tutorial): www.youtube.com/watch?v=0KGOUSf96C4
- Edmodo app information: itunes.apple.com/us/app/edmodo/id378352300?mt=8
- EdmodoCon 2013 recordings, photos, and more!: blog.edmodo.com/2013/08/15/best-of-edmodocon-2013/
- Webinars and video tutorials: support.edmodo.com/home-entries/22006035-webinars
- Teacher and parent guides (PDFs)—Scottsdale Unified School District: 484help.susd.schoolfusion.us/modules/groups/group_pages.phtml?gid=1029155&nid=305309

—m—

Schoology
Schoology, Inc.
Website: www.schoology.com/
Cost: Free; also available on Android
Schoology was developed in 2010 but has been increasing in popularity in recent years. This app and associated website provide a free learning manage-

ment system (LMS). Of course, it does not have all the bells and whistles of Blackboard and other paid LMSs. Regardless it has much to offer, including:

1. Assignment areas
2. Tests/quizzes
3. Files/links
4. Discussion areas
5. Albums
6. Pages for instruction

Individual teachers may use this site. However, many schools are now using it to track student attendance and grades. Further information for Schoology is limited here because plenty of tutorials exist; a few are provided below. However, Figure 2.8 shows an example of a physics classroom.

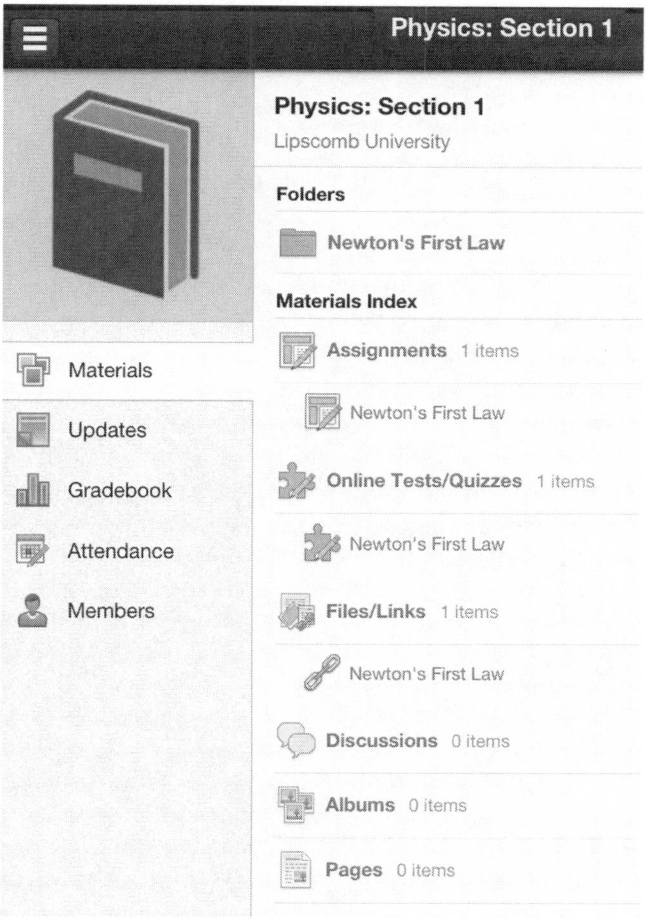

Figure 2.8.   Course material

Folders provide the information available for individual lessons or sections. Additional material can be added, as shown by the links below the folder.

For students to sign up, they simply need to start on the Schoology home page, then click on Sign up and then on Student. Here is where they need to type in the access code that their teachers have provided. The next screen asks them for their names and to set up user names and passwords. Once students have joined classes, teachers are notified by email. If needed, teachers can easily remove students from any classes.

Sampling of Videos and Websites with Edmodo Information
- Basic Schoology tutorial: www.youtube.com/watch?v=4zvQA41eDCE
- Schoology tutorial: www.youtube.com/watch?v=fbEBtHGnAyU
- Using Google Documents with Schoology: www.sophia.org/using-google -documents-with-schoology-tutorial

Reflections on Chapter 2

By becoming comfortable with the nine apps that are covered in this chapter, educators can significantly increase the instructional possibilities! Teachers are thus poised to have entirely new classrooms, where the students are engaged and actively learning. Students look forward to coming to a class where true learning is taking place. We have all heard that the majority of our students are visual learners. Timothy Gangwer (2009) wrote that "[s]ixty-five percent of our students are visual learners." The built-in Camera and Photos apps, along with Text on Photo, can go a long way to engage the visual learner.

With the presentation apps, teachers have a variety of ways to present material. Using PowerPoint day in and day out usually leads to glazed-over eyes, even for those students who manage to stay awake. Teachers can surprise their students with the new look of a Prezi presentation! However, even Prezi can become tiresome if teachers use it regularly. Variety remains an essential ingredient of quality teaching. Teachers should limit the number of classroom presentations. At least occasionally, they should use Educreations to share material through a flipped classroom environment.

With Evernote, users can suddenly organize all their thoughts! What an asset for the chaotic world of teaching! Furthermore, teachers have a free way in which students can create digital portfolios. Then who can possibly deny the value of using Dropbox? Its ability to nearly instantaneously sync all files puts this app on a pedestal above most all other apps. As far as social learning platforms, Edmodo tops all other current competitors. This app allows for the sharing of material and ideas with students, parents, and colleagues.

After becoming comfortable with the nine apps covered in this chapter and applying them, educators may discover that it is not only the students who are more engaged. Teachers may develop a new spark of enthusiasm that was lost in years past. Stay tuned now. Chapter 3 has even more highly ranked apps that can also be used across all subject areas.

CHAPTER THREE

—◦◦◦—

Apps and Techniques for All Subject Areas, Part 2

Introduction

Chapter 2 covered nine apps that have tremendous value for all subject areas. This chapter contains fourteen more apps that also offer substantial value for educators. Readers may rightly wonder why the nine were placed in chapter 2, while others were relegated to this chapter. Consider, if you will, the analogy of using an iPad to be like viewing a Broadway play. The nine apps in the previous chapter could be considered the "principal actors" in this "performance" of using the iPad to enhance the role of educators. The key actors have prominent positions throughout the play.

Other featured roles in a play are critical to the story, but their appearance is not quite as regular. Apps that can be considered as the key actors are described in chapter 2 because those are the apps that teachers might use on a fairly regular basis, whereas the fourteen apps in this chapter should be considered the actors with featured roles. Their roles are critical, but the apps may not be used as regularly as the ones in the previous chapter. Of course, some teachers might value some of these even above those in the previous chapter. So read through the descriptions of each of these apps, making your own value assessments.

Regardless, do not underestimate the value of these fourteen apps. Each one of these is well known for having a valued place in today's classrooms. Readers should not try to absorb all of them at once. Slowly exploring each of them should be both exciting and beneficial.

Quiz Maker and Game Apps

Does it seem odd that "quiz" and "game" are included in the same category? Historically, those two words were almost considered to be antonyms. Until recently, teachers would have never thought that there was even a remote relationship between a quiz and a game. Gradually, student assessments have begun to sometimes incorporate gaming techniques, especially for pretest review sessions.

One personally devised game divided a geometry class into three teams. Each team was given three-meter sticks and two small circular clamps. After drawing a card with a name of "alternate interior," "corresponding," and so on, one member of each team would have to place his or her sticks and clamps in the correct position. A correct answer would temporarily retire the card. An incorrect answer would bring all the cards back to the original pile. The first team to have all of their members correctly place the objects would be the winner. By the end of the game, most of the students confidently knew the various types of angles.

Jeopardy was another game that began to be played in the classroom in the early 1990s. Soon Jeopardy software was developed, saving teachers from having to draw their own charts. Today, an app for Jeopardy is now available, although it is not included in this book; many other game apps seem to offer so much more.

In recent years, the term "gamification" has become an accepted term within the world of education. A *Forbes* magazine article defined the term as "applying game-design thinking to non-game applications to make them more fun and engaging." The article began, "It is human nature to play. . . . Play enables us to explore new things, to stretch our abilities, to learn and adapt" (Swann, 2012).

Classrooms should always be about learning and adapting. Considerable research confirms the benefits of using games in the classroom. A recent article titled "8 Research Findings Supporting the Benefits of Gamification in Education" discussed research findings from around the world that showed over and over the benefits of using games in the classroom (Walsh, 2012).

Many games are available in subject-specific apps, and some of those are discussed in later chapters. Below are two apps that can be used across all subject areas. One website includes the following statement: "Games in the hands of a skilled and experienced teacher can achieve magical results" (Tawse, 2009).

—*e/e/e*—

Teacher Clicker—Socrative
Socrative
Website: itunes.apple.com/us/app/teacher-clicker-socrative/id477620120
Cost: Free; also available on Android

Socrative is a *fun* way for teachers to facilitate discussions, to assess understanding prior to teaching a new topic, or to quickly determine learning after covering the topic. The quizzes can be set up solely online, as well as on the iPad, although as always the directions here focus solely on iPad usage. When signing up for Socrative, you will be alerted to the fact that "[y]ou need at least 2 devices to try Socrative." The devices can be any combination of computer, iPad, iPhone, or iPod Touch.

When there are a limited number of devices, Socrative does allow multiple students to submit answers from a single device. As soon as teachers create accounts, they are assigned a room number. Students who are using a laptop simply need to type in the address m.socrative.com. Students on other devices need to download the free Student Clicker—Socrative app. When they have opened Socrative, students first need to write in the room number that their teachers provide. Teachers' pages always show the number of students who have entered the "room."

Teachers can choose one of six tools, as shown in Figure 3.1. With the multiple-choice question, students can see only the five buttons to use to select A, B, C, D, or E. Teachers can choose to say the question with possible answers, display everything on the board, or provide a handout with the possible answers. Once each student logs into the room and submits the answer, a bar chart immediately appears on teachers' screens. Teachers can save the chart with the standard iPad screen-save option of simultaneously hitting the on–off button and the home button.

The picture can be retrieved at any time from the iPad's Camera Roll. When teachers hit the End activity button, the Activity screen appears again. The true/false questions work similarly, with students being given only two options. For short-answer questions, students write in their answers and then tap the Submit button. Teachers can then see a list of all the answers. Teachers can tap on the Vote on Responses button. This allows the answers to be viewable to all of the students, with the names hidden. Then the students can vote on the best answer.

When teachers tap on Start Quiz, students can begin to answer questions from a database of quizzes that teachers have set up. At the completion of

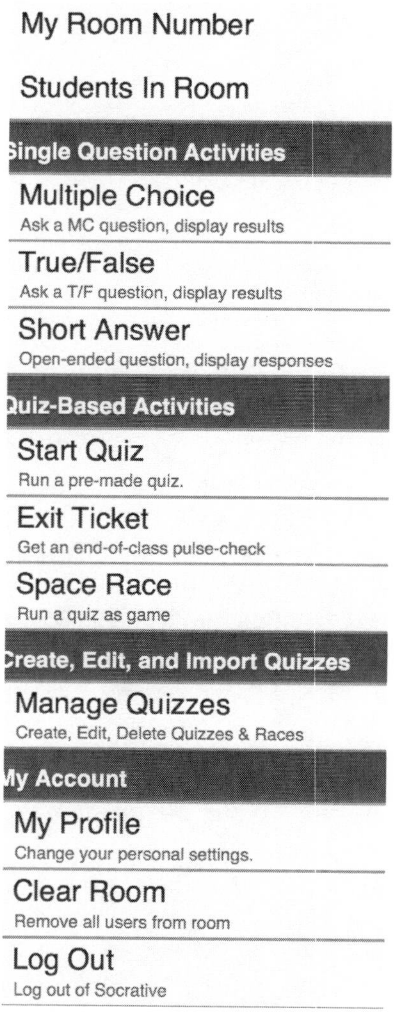

My Room Number

Students In Room

Single Question Activities

Multiple Choice
Ask a MC question, display results

True/False
Ask a T/F question, display results

Short Answer
Open-ended question, display responses

Quiz-Based Activities

Start Quiz
Run a pre-made quiz.

Exit Ticket
Get an end-of-class pulse-check

Space Race
Run a quiz as game

Create, Edit, and Import Quizzes

Manage Quizzes
Create, Edit, Delete Quizzes & Races

My Account

My Profile
Change your personal settings.

Clear Room
Remove all users from room

Log Out
Log out of Socrative

Figure 3.1. Socrative menu

the quiz, teachers receive emailed spreadsheets, with detailed reports on the results. While giving the quiz, teachers have the option to make the quiz student paced or teacher paced. At any point during the quiz, teachers can tap on the Live Results bar and see exactly who is taking the quiz, as well as the number of answers that each student has answered correctly.

Making a quiz is quite intuitive. However, teachers also have the option to import either a shared quiz or the template of a quiz. For the shared quiz, the SOC number (Socrative number) is needed, which other teachers may have made available. For importing quizzes from an Excel template, teachers need to work through a browser, not just the app.

Figure 3.1 also shows a Space Race option. This is where gaming and fun really come into play. Teachers can select a quiz, as they do in the quiz section, but now they also have the option of selecting up to ten teams. Students then compete against each other. During the quiz, teachers can project the results so students can watch the small rockets moving across the board. After the quiz has been finished, teachers receive reports in the same way they did for the other, more formal quiz. Elementary and high school students alike love competing in this way also.

Another outstanding feature of Socrative is the Exit Ticket. This allows teachers to design their own templates or to use an Exit Ticket template, designed by Socrative. Thus, teachers can quickly assess student understanding from the day's lesson. More information is available from the second link below. In 2013, Socrative added two new features. Images can now be added to multiple-choice and short-answer questions. Also, teachers have the option to add answers to short-answer questions and then let the system grade the answers.

Sampling of Websites with Socrative Information
- Socrative Smart Student Response System: www.socrative.com/how-it-works
- Socrative Exit Ticket and Space Race: www.youtube.com/watch?v=0w NnVUKVIAc

—~~—

Quizzam!
Griffin Technology
Website: store.griffintechnology.com/quizzam-buzzer-app-for-ipad-ipod-iphone
Cost: $0.99

Ten years ago, many schools were purchasing sets of expensive game-buzzer systems that teachers could check out and use in their classrooms. Quizzam! is a student-response app that replaces the need to invest the several hundred dollars in that hardware. This app is much more intuitive than similar apps that are available. It does require that teachers and students all have their settings set on the same Wi-Fi network. Once teachers have downloaded and opened the app, they simply give the class a name and a password and then tap the Create button.

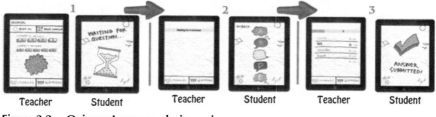

Figure 3.2.   Quizzam! screens, during quiz

On the next screen, the ???Questions button, in the lower right corner, should be selected. This opens a screen that allows teachers to choose the option of Buzz In or Mult. Choice. Students who have downloaded the Quizzam! app must be on the same Wi-Fi network as their teachers are. When they open the app and select that they are a Student, they are asked for a name; they should tap the blue Login button. Students then need to type in the password that teachers provided, and their screens go to the Waiting for Question screen, as shown in Figure 3.2. If, as the students wait, the teacher selects the Mult. Choice option, then the teacher also needs to specify the number of possible answers and which answer is correct.

Teachers can provide handouts or show the questions on a board or project them on a screen. When all is set, teachers then tap on the big blue Quizzam! button, in the center of the screen. As shown in the middle section of Figure 3.2, teachers wait as the students ponder whether to select A, B, C, or D. Obviously, if teachers pick only two or three answers, students will be shown only two or three options. The images on the right side show that the student has answered the question. Teachers' screens show the names of the students who answered, the answers the students provided, and the amount of time the students took to respond to the questions. Selecting the Buzz In option of this app allows teachers to play any number of games in which teams are asked to buzz in before answering a question. As the students buzz in, teachers see the list of students or teams in the order of who buzzed in the quickest.

Quizzam! is an excellent way for teachers to assess learning at the end of any class discussion! Students view this app as a fun way to be tested. The app also allows teachers to keep track of who is still engaged in the activity. Thus, teachers can immediately address any problems with students who might be trying to check their phone messages during class sessions. The statement from the promo video provided below states that Quizzam! is "the simpler, more engaging way to quiz your students."

Website with Quizzam! Information
- Quizzam! makes testing and quizzes using your iPad, iPhone or iPod touch—YouTube video with good overview: www.youtube.com/watch?v=zKU7EI7cww8

Enhance Learning with Audio

Readers may ask "Why on earth would an educator need two apps for generating audio files?" That is a very valid question. The short answer is that each of these apps has substantially different capabilities. The AudioMemos app comes the closest to being a pure audio file generator. However, the Dragon Dictation app is a speech-to-text application. They both have earned high recommendations and deserve to be considered by every teacher.

—⁓—

AudioMemos—The Voice Recorder
Imesart 5.1.r.l.
Website: imesart.com/products.php?pid=1
Cost: $0.99; also available on Android

A search in the App Store for "voice recorder" brings up a seemingly endless collection of voice-recording apps. This app deserves attention, above all other voice-recorder apps. In fact, the first article in the collection of websites below claims that this is the best voice recorder for the iPad. The app is easy to work with, and the recordings are loud and of excellent quality.

Additionally, it is easy to transfer the files. There are actually three versions of this app: free, $0.99, and $9.99. The free version allows files only up to 3 MB to be mailed, whereas 15 MB is allowed for both of the other versions. The ability to send larger files more than justifies the $0.99 fee. Other features that differentiate the three versions are clearly listed on the first website below.

The opening screen provides a big red Record button, at the bottom of the screen. To create an audio file, users simply tap on that button and talk for a minute or less, speaking clearly and naturally. At any time, users can use the Pause button. When finished, users can test the recording to see whether it is acceptable. During playback users can stop the recording and again tap Play to overwrite any part of the recording. Also users can add more to the recording by hitting the Record button again at the end of what was previously recorded. When finished, users should tap the Done button, at the top.

Tapping on the Audio Memos button, at the top left, brings up a list of all the files. If users hold the iPad horizontally, the list shows automatically. To delete any specific file, users tap on the Edit button, at the top, and then tap on the minus sign, to the left of the file's title. To change the title of a file, users simply open the file and tap on the Edit button, at the top right. Then they tap in the title area. By default the file is always given a title of the date and time of the recording. Tapping on the little "x" in the title area deletes the title, allowing users to type a new title. Users tap Done, in the upper right, to finish and save the new title.

The value of this app is that the generated audio files can be used in multiple ways. After users tap the Done button, the red Record button changes to a blue Send button. Then, selecting the Send button opens a new window, with options for Email or More. Tapping More brings up the option to select App, which provides the option to send the file to other apps that users have loaded on the iPad, such as Edmodo, Dropbox, Schoology, Evernote, Documents, and iMovie.

This app then is great for verbally recording information for later use. Also, teachers can use it for a flipped classroom, requiring students to listen to information prior to class. Recordings of lectures or interviews can also be saved.

Sampling of Websites with Audio Memos Information
- Audio Memos for iPhone and iPad review: The best voice recorder app for the iPad—discusses the app and also compares the three versions: www.imore.com/audio-memos-iphone-ipad-review-voice-recorder-app-ipad
- Audio Memos—a voice recorder for iPad & iPhone: This article includes a video tutorial that uses the Pro account on the iPhone. However, it has some useful details that apply to the iPad app that, because of space limitations, were not able to be included here. The paid features are explained at the very end of the video: www.freetech4teachers.com/2012/03/audio-memos-voice-recorder-for-ipad.html#.UQ0dDdWG6So

———

Dragon Dictation
Nuance Communication
Website: www.nuancemobilelife.com/
Cost: Free

This paragraph is being brought to you courtesy of Dragon Dictation. What does that mean? It means that this app allows users to dictate something to the iPad, which then is automatically turned into typed text! That written record can then easily be emailed, copied, or sent to Facebook. So, the words in this paragraph were never typed. They were merely spoken to an iPad, using Dragon Dictation, then emailed, and finally copied and pasted onto this page.

The app is known as a speech-to-text application, and it does require network access to work. But what fun! For the previous paragraph, I simply opened the app on my iPad and tapped on the red button below the words "Tap and dictate." After speaking those words and tapping on the screen (anywhere), the typed words automatically appeared on the screen. Although not always perfect, this app is usually very accurate.

The only correction that needed to be made in the first paragraph was that I forgot to say "period" at the end of the last sentence. "Exclamation mark" and "question mark" were dictated correctly as needed. Also the word "cap" was spoken prior to "Dragon" and again prior to "Dictation" so that those words would be capitalized. The forgotten period was added by tapping on the little keyboard icon at the bottom, center of the screen; that brings up the keyboard so that any corrections or additions can be made.

With each text, there are three options, as shown on the top-right menu bar. The plus sign allows users to add additional words to what was already recorded. The trash can is for deleting the note. Then the third icon provides the following six options: email, cut, copy, Facebook, Twitter, and settings.

Sample Website with Dragon Dictation Information
- iPad and Dragon Dictation—This video was made in 2010, so there are some differences from the current version, but it is still very good and gives some excellent explanations: www.youtube.com/watch?v=ymxs D4MGKLI

Video Conferencing

The value of field experiences cannot be overstated. Many teachers are unwilling to endure the ordeal of making arrangements at the site, scheduling transportation, collecting any necessary money from students, checking the free and reduced lunch lists for the students who got to go free, and finally collecting permission slips signed by the parents and teachers of each student. Yet, seeing students become acquainted with something that was outside of their often-limited sphere of experiences always makes the trip well worth the effort.

However, primarily because of budget cuts, restrictions on field experiences are continually growing. Here comes video conferencing to the rescue!

Teachers can bring guest speakers to the classroom through the "eye" of an iPad. Some speakers can give tours of remote sites that would not be feasible for the students to travel to.

Groups of students can have discussions with classes in schools at remote sites. The College of Education at Lipscomb University regularly schedules Skype sessions with classes at a school in Lima, Peru. The Peruvian teachers want their students to have the experience of speaking English, and it benefits our university students to learn about the Peruvian culture.

FaceTime is the video-conferencing app that automatically comes on iPads, so readers may ask why it is not included in the discussion here. The primary reason is that FaceTime works only with other FaceTime users, which limits it to iPads or other Mac devices. FaceTime is intuitive and generates excellent-quality videos. However, Skype definitely reaches out to a wider range of users.

⟶⟵

Skype
Skype Communications SARL
Website: skype.com
Cost: Free; also available on Android

Before using the app, users need to set up a Skype account at the website above. Opening the app for the first time requires a log-in with user name and password. After the first time, logging in is done automatically. The next screen shows all the contacts that are associated with users. Obviously, if users are new to Skype, that screen is just waiting for contacts to be added, which can be started by first tapping on the plus symbol on the top right of the screen. Next, there are two ways to locate a Skype contact. Users can choose to search a Skype directory by typing in a name, email address, or Skype name.

Users can also add a contact by adding a specific phone number. An email is always sent out to the individual first, asking permission to be a contact. To initiate a call, users tap on a contact; then, on the next screen, they select the green Video Call button. An alternative way is to simply tap on the collection of dots that appear on the top bar, just to the left of the plus symbol. Those dots represent a phone keypad, which is exactly what comes up when the dots are tapped. Users simply tap out the number on that keypad. The second website listed below visually steps users through the same directions that are provided here.

Skype is perfect for giving live tours of museums, zoos, parks, or other locations. When using Skype in a classroom, teachers may prefer to show the class on the screen. That can be done by using the rear-facing camera, which is accessed by tapping at the bottom of the screen to bring up the icon of the camera. That icon serves as a toggle switch between the forward- and rear-facing cameras. For example, a classroom may want the docent of the museum to see the students, so the rear-facing camera would be appropriate for that.

In another case, when teachers are running sessions between two classrooms, the rear-facing camera might be used through most of the session. For science teachers, students could collect field data from different places around the world and then have discussions about their findings with other distant classrooms. With this app, teachers can also discuss topics with absent or homebound students. Skype has tremendous potential for collaborative work with other teachers. The collection of websites below provides innumerable ideas on how educators have used Skype to enhance the learning experiences of their students.

Sampling of Websites with Skype Information
- Skype for iPad: Avoid FaceTime's one-to-one limitation: www.informationweek.com/byte/personal-tech/mobile-applications/skype-for-ipad-avoid-facetimes-one-to-on/231400059
- Skype on the iPad 2 overview tutorial—clearly shows two iPads during a Skype session: www.youtube.com/watch?v=4C0QI429cw0
- Connect your classroom to the world—Start by watching two introductory videos: education.skype.com/
- Cool ways to use Skype in the classroom—one teacher's perspective, with lots of associated links: www.teachhub.com/using-skype-classroom
- Skype an author network—a wiki that organizes how to connect with authors who would be willing to Skype to your classroom: skypeanauthor.wikifoundry.com
- The Mixxer—a free educational website for language exchanges via Skype—This site is for both students and teachers of language learners to connect with other language learners around the world: language-exchanges.org/

Annotate Shapes, Images, and Videos

Remember the ease with which the Text on Photo app, described in the previous chapter, can be used to type text onto images? Well, the app below also allows annotation of images. In addition, this app has a few added tools that allow users to annotate virtually anything that can be pulled up on the iPad screen.

⟶⟨⟩⟶

Skitch
Evernote
Website: evernote.com/skitch/
Cost: Free; also available on Android

Teachers and students alike love the creativity that this app allows. It could be accurately designated as "a free annotate-anything-for-any-subject-or-any-topic app." That is, users can add a variety of annotations to any video or photo, as well as a vast array of shapes. Additionally, users can annotate any portion of a web page and save it as a graphic! The app is also easy to share, and since the makers of Evernote created it, the annotated images automatically sync to Evernote accounts.

Skitch requires having an Evernote account. Then, when first opening Skitch, users are asked whether they want to "Create an Evernote notebook named 'Skitch' for your Skitch Notes." This is certainly recommended, although it can be changed later. Tapping on the plus sign in the main area opens a window with six options:

- Take a photo
- Choose a photo
- Create from PDF
- Draw on map
- Start with blank
- Capture from the web

Tapping on Choose a Photo takes users to the Photo Roll, where they can make any selection. When they select an image, the menu bar appears, as shown on the right side of Figure 3.3. The words "'Swimming' Backstroke" were done with Skitch.

The other words were added to the snapshot of the image to identify the menu tools. Altogether the menu provides eight primary tools:

1. Draw an arrow, with the head of the arrow at the end.
2. Type text—the keyboard automatically comes up when users tap the screen
3. Draw a line or one of three types of borders around an area.
4. Use a virtual felt marker either to draw with or to highlight an area.
5. Select the color, shade, and intensity for all the previous options.
6. Blur a selected area.
7. Crop an area.
8. Add one of five stamps: red with an x, yellow with an exclamation mark, blue with a question mark, green with a check mark, or red with a heart.

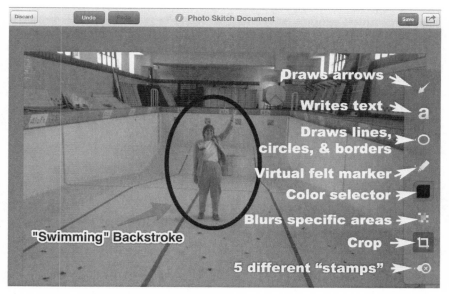

Figure 3.3. Sample image with labeled menu

After users have completed and saved an image, it is placed in the Skitch Notes area, which always syncs with users' Evernote sites. Instead of selecting an image from the iPad's Photo area, users can Capture from Web. The Skitch website opens as the default page; users can change the URL address to any active web page. When users have located the desired website, they tap on the Snap button, at the bottom-right corner, to bring up the standard menu, as shown in Figure 3.3.

The sites below include a Skitch tutorial, as well as an article that provides specific ways to use Skitch in the classroom.

Sampling of Websites with Skitch Information
- Demo of Skitch app for iPad: www.youtube.com/watch?v=f1I7Y-Zjd_w
- Using Skitch in your classroom: reflectandrefine.blogspot.com/2012/07/using-skitch-in-your-classroom.html

Presentation-Assisting Apps

The two apps in this section are substantially different from each other, yet they both can be used to enhance a classroom presentation. iPrompt Pro serves as a teleprompter, whereas BrainPop comes with an immense collection of built-in videos.

⎯⎯

i-Prompt Pro
OurApps4U Limited
Website: www.i-prompter.com
Cost: Free; also available on Android

In a report published by the American Federation of Teachers, Dr. Louisa Moats wrote, "Teaching reading IS rocket science" (1999). Teaching reading, at all grade levels, can be very complex. However, this app helps to develop confidence for students at all reading levels. iPrompt Pro is, very simply, a teleprompter that can be adjusted with font size and speed according to the needs of the speaker. The prompter could be used in any class in which students are giving presentations.

The welcome page for the app provides "a few instructions on how to use it." However, while those directions are accurate, they may be hard to follow for first-time users. The steps below add some additional details:

1. Tap on the iPrompt Pro icon. During the commercial for the remotes, just tap the screen or wait. A second commercial may come up. If so, tap the back button, at the top left, to return to the main screen.

2. Start to become familiar with the Settings area, which can be accessed by tapping on the Settings button, at the top left. Choices are provided for customizing the fonts and background colors, as well as the speed and orientation of the prompt. Setting the speed correctly is very important when working with students. Certainly English language learners and younger students need far slower speeds. The default setting for Auto Start is Yes, although most teachers find it more useful to turn that off. Also, if a remote is not available, turn the Remote Type to none to avoid an annoying pop-up, which states that no remote is available.

3. To set up a document, simply tap on the plus button, at the right of the top menu. On the next window, type in a Title. Then either type or paste in the Document Text. Teachers may want their students to copy their own documents or copy famous historic speeches from the web.

4. Save when everything is set.

5. Tapping on the Share icon (curved arrow) brings up a menu with four choices: Start (for beginning the teleprompter), Edit (for editing the text), Copy, or Delete (for deleting the entire document). When START is tapped, the prompter starts scrolling automatically unless users have turned off that Auto Start feature. If the Auto Start is off, the scrolling will not start until the little arrow at the top is selected.

6. To stop the scrolling, just double tap the screen. Users then have the capability to scroll through the document or to tap the Share icon, at the top, to return to the main menu.

The importance of improving reading capabilities has always been recognized as one of the most important goals of the educational system. The article from Edutopia, listed below, stated, "This app will offer a meaningful reason for students to develop reading fluency." This applies to early childhood, as well as to special education and ELL classrooms.

Sampling of Websites with iPrompt Pro Information
- iPrompt Pro tutorial: www.youtube.com/watch?v=V9RR8FjqV9E
- K–5 iPad apps for applying: Bloom's Revised Taxonomy, Part 3: www
  .edutopia.org/blog/ipad-apps-elementary-blooms-taxomony-applying
  -diane-darrow

—*www*—

BrainPOP
BrainPOP
Website: www.brainpop.com
Cost: Free for a limited portion; also available on Android
This app is incredible! Another must-have! Unfortunately, the full version of this app comes with considerable expense. However, some free options are available. BrainPOP was founded in 1997 by a pediatrician who wanted to explain medical procedures to his young patients. The company has now expanded to over one thousand animated videos for K–12 students, in almost all subject areas. In 2010, BrainPOP was quick to come aboard with a quality app.

With each video, teachers can ask students to take the associated quiz and then have access to the individual scores. Also, with each video, there are links provided to a collection of related videos. The subjects are categorized as follows:

- Science
- Social studies
- English
- Reading and writing
- Math
- Engineering and technology
- Health
- Arts and music

BrainPOP originally focused on grades 5 and above. However, there is now a BrainPOP Jr., which offers videos appropriate for K–3 classrooms. Almost without exception, students love it! Each video features a young man, Tim, and his associate, a robot named Moby. For each topic, teachers can retrieve printable handouts, including lesson plans. A good starting place for this app is to watch BrainPOP's tour, which is provided in the first link below.

There are actually two BrainPOP apps that are currently free. The first is BrainPOP Featured Movie, which regularly provides movies with related material for older students. Similarly, BrainPOP Jr. Movie of the Week runs a different movie each week. Students look forward to those movies, but teachers, of course, first need to check to see how well they fit into the curriculum.

The second site below provides all of the various fee structures. The best option is for a school district, or at least the school, to sign up for BrainPOP. Classroom teachers can sign up for an annual fee of about $200. This is fairly reasonable, considering all of the material that is included. However, the best option is for principals or district administrators to be informed of the benefits, and hopefully one of them will agree to sign up. BrainPOP videos have tremendous value for enhancing learning in the classroom.

There are some other free resources available from BrainPOP at an educator's site. The last two links below explain those options.

Sampling of Websites with BrainPOP Information
- BrainPOP tour—covers all key areas: www.brainpop.com/about/tour/
- Subscribe—Starting point to find fees for signing up for the full version: secure.brainpop.com/store/step1/
- BrainPOP free stuff—truly free: www.brainpop.com/free_stuff/
- BrainPOP educators—free, even if you've not signed up for the paid version: www.brainpop.com/educators

Teacher Tools

Large school systems often pay large fees to set up systems for teachers to record grades and take attendance. The single app in this section can do that for free. It addition, it has many more valuable features for classroom teachers, including being able to take attendance, without having to call out a single student's name!

TeacherKit
ITWorx Egypt SAE
Website: teacherkit.net/
Cost: Free

Originally known as TeacherPal, this app changed its name in 2012 to reflect the additional features that were being included. Teachers can use this app to organize their classroom, with features for recording grades and keeping attendance. Grades can be imported and exported from other programs. In addition, teachers can set up seating charts that easily can be rearranged at any time.

Teachers can take attendance right on the seating chart by just noticing what seats are vacant and set up and easily maintain student contact information. Assuming that teachers receive parental permission, they can take a picture of each student, which can then be associated with the student's information within this app. Teachers can also create class email lists.

A feature that will really catch teachers' attention is how easy it is to record incidents of misbehavior. A standard cry of principals is for their teachers to "document, document, document!" With this app, teachers can quickly note a record of misbehavior, without taking time to type a document on a computer. Indeed, there are many features for one free app! The first website below includes the statement "The only thing it doesn't do is teach the class for you." This may be a bit of an exaggeration, but this app can be very useful for most teachers.

Tapping on the plus sign, on the left of the top bar, as shown by the arrow in Figure 3.4, begins the process of setting up a new class. Initially, entering the title of the class is all that is critical. As more classes are added, they are arranged in alphabetical order. If teachers tap on the Edit button, on the top right of the screen, the class doors begin to jiggle. Tapping on one of the doors brings up four new icons on the top left, as soon as users' fingers are removed.

First, the pencil allows teachers to add or edit the description of the class. Also there is the Timetable Mode, which is a setting that allows teachers to Manage Lessons and set grading periods. The trash can is the next icon, allowing teachers to delete a class. The up and down arrows provide a way for teachers to export or import information. For example, tapping on the up arrow allows teachers to export data, such as Student Roster, Grades, Attendance, Behavior, or Gradebook Templates.

Users can select which areas to export and then select either iTunes or email. The files are transferred either as zip files or cvs files. The Roster is always exported as a zip file. When opened, it shows all the students' pictures and an Excel sheet of their contact information. Similarly, the grade book can be exported as an Excel sheet. Tapping on one of the doors brings up a close-up view of the door, along with the Class Description. To begin to

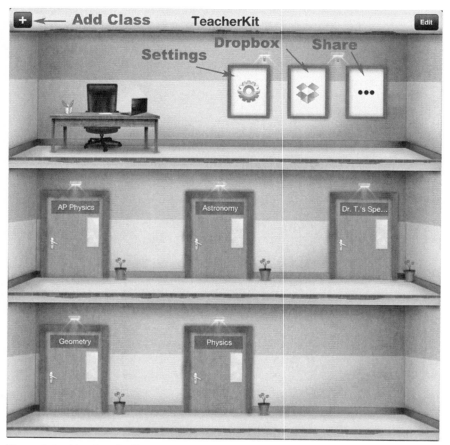

Figure 3.4. TeacherKit Classes

add information to the class, teachers can tap anywhere on the large door to enter the class and then tap on the plus icon on the upper right.

The drop-down menu provides four choices for adding students:

- Add new student
- Add from contacts
- Face detection
- Add from other classes

Face Detection allows a fun method of simply using a class picture, in which the pictures can be identified, and on the next screen, names can be added. After the students are entered, teachers can use the main features of this app: Attendance, Behavior, and Gradebook. Little circles indicate the number of absences.

This app provides many other features that can assist teachers in their daily classroom routines. For additional information, readers are referred to some of the online tutorials that are available at the websites listed below. Teachers can certainly use just the basics initially and then add features later as time allows and needs arise.

Sampling of YouTube Videos with TeacherKit Information
- TeacherKit: www.youtube.com/watch?v=JJF2inmZFjA
- TeacherKit video—how the app has changed a teacher's life: www.youtube.com/watch?v=pbfkG6YTyqQ

Free Professional Development

Throughout the K–12 environment, some poorly planned professional development sessions can be exceedingly painful! In addition to being incredibly boring, some are also totally irrelevant to the attendees' areas of teaching. A professional development session should always fulfill one or both of two essential purposes. First, sessions should provide new knowledge and skills that can be applied for immediate use. Second, the sessions should inspire and encourage educators to move beyond the mundane and to continue to find excitement within their profession.

The three apps in this session allow educators to search for topics that are relevant to their area. Each of these apps provides quality sessions that inspire and encourage. Often, the information provides short videos that teachers can share directly with their students.

⸺⸺⸺

Khan Academy
Salman Khan
Website: www.khanacademy.org/
Cost: Free; also available on Android

Hopefully, most readers have already heard of this app! If daily routines and training on the current standards have cheated you out of knowing about Khan Academy, then take some time soon and allow yourself the luxury of being absorbed into watching some videos from this app's tremendous collection of over 3,200 free videos! Topics span the gamut of most school subjects.

The first website, listed below, suggests being very specific when searching for topics. That is, do not search for math or even algebra. Rather search for topics such as linear equations or the Vietnam War. However, users can search by subject area from links provided on the home screen. All the videos can be used for professional development, or they can be projected from an iPad to be shared with a class. The videos are not usually geared for elementary students but are fantastic for high school– and university-level teachers.

Sampling of Websites with Khan Academy Information, Tutorials, or Help Forums

- Khan Academy's iPad app—breaking news: www.khanacademy.org/about/blog/post/24905749288/ipad-app
- About Khan Academy: www.khanacademy.org/about
- Let's use video to reinvent education—from Salman Khan himself: www.ted.com/talks/salman_khan_let_s_use_video_to_reinvent_education.html

—⁓—

iTunes U
Apple, Inc.
Website: www.apple.com/apps/itunes-u/
Cost: Free

The iTunes U site promises that the app offers "more than 500,000 free lectures, videos, books, and other resources on thousands of subjects." The lectures originally came from a small collection of elite colleges and universities. Now, more than three hundred colleges and universities have submitted videos, and recently K–12 institutions have also begun to participate, with significant submissions. When first opening this app, there is an empty bookcase with a note that "[y]ou can browse or subscribe to free courses in the iTunes U catalog." Users can start browsing by tapping on the Catalog button, on the top left of the bookcase.

Users should then notice the Search area, in the upper-right corner. Users can simply type a topic of interest there, and a vast array of resources will likely come. For example, typing in "Abraham Lincoln" brings up resources sorted into four major areas:

- iTunes U Episodes
- iTunes U Collections
- iTunes U Materials
- iTunes U Courses

A search for a more specific topic, such as "solving systems of linear equations," did not bring up quite as many resources, but there were still five collections and twenty-five episodes. The collections included the specific episodes, as well as a whole collection of other algebraic topics. Users can download video and audio files, as well as printable handouts. The first three websites below provide excellent information for maneuvering around this app. Teachers should regularly search for and use these resources to fill up that bookcase! Also, teachers should check out the last website below for an overview for how to create their own course in iTunes U.

Sampling of Websites with iTunes U Information, Tutorials, or Help Forums
- Five things that could make Apple's new iTunes U a winner: reviews .cnet.com/8301-31747_7-57362307-243/five-things-that-could-make -apples-new-itunes-u-a-winner/
- Get smarter with iTunes U: www.macworld.com/article/1163267/ get_smarter_with_itunes_u.html
- iTunes U frequently asked questions: support.apple.com/kb/HT5100
- Create your own custom course on iTunes U: www.apple.com/support/ itunes-u/docs/course_guidelines/

—————

TED
TED Conferences
Website: www.ted.com/
Cost: Free; also available on Android

This app offers an immense collection of intriguing talks that should inspire any educator. The talks are all from TED's biannual conferences. Below are a few quotes from the TED website that explain the mission of this organization:

- TED is a nonprofit devoted to Ideas Worth Spreading. It started out (in 1984) as a conference bringing together people from three worlds: Technology, Entertainment, and Design.
- The conferences . . . bring together the world's most fascinating thinkers and doers, who are challenged to give the talk of their lives (in 18 minutes or less).
- More than 1400 TED Talks are now available, with more added each week.
- We believe passionately in the power of ideas to change attitudes, lives and ultimately, the world.

This app has the power to rejuvenate even the uninspired. The opening screen shows Featured Talks. Users can toggle to see those by tapping on the up and down arrows, shown on the top menu bar. One of the videos on that screen undoubtedly will continue to be a talk, given in 2006, by Sir Ken Robinson, titled "Schools Kill Creativity." Over fifteen million viewers have watched that video; it is a must-see for all educators.

The topics of these talks are not as subject specific as the previous two apps are. However, they have the capability to inspire even educators that may be suffering from a bit of burnout. They are also great for stimulating class discussions. On the TED website, the left menu bar has categories such as Most Viewed, Funny, and Science, among others. That bar is missing from the iPad, but searches are always possible from the menu bar, at the bottom, as shown in Figure 3.5.

Be aware that a search for as broad a subject as algebra will most likely come up empty. Remember, the focus of TED is to inspire and stimulate rather than to offer any specific instructions. "Mathematics" will come up with half a dozen talks that would be appropriate for high school classrooms or for professional development. The talks include "The mathematics of war," "The mathematics of history," and "Teaching kids real math with computers."

An excellent method for discovering valuable talks is to tap on the All Talks area. The videos there are sorted by themes, one of which is "How We Learn." Currently, fifty videos are listed within that area. Every video on TED can be shared, bookmarked, or saved. When users tap on Save, occasionally an option to "Save audio," as well as "Save video for offline viewing," will be provided.

Videos are generally more valuable for classroom purposes, as most students are visual learners. However, the audio does save a lot of iPad memory space. Saved videos take up a lot of memory on the iPad, but then they can be easily accessed from tapping on the My Talks star, on the menu bar.

In March 2012, TED launched a new area of TED, called TEDED. The focus of this new venture is to use TED videos to create and share lesson

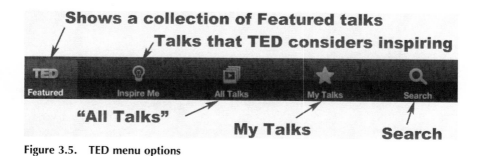

Figure 3.5.   TED menu options

plans through a flipped classroom. This feature currently is not available on the app, although the videos can be found on the TED app by doing a search for "TEDED". The fourth site listed below has more information.

Sampling of Websites with TED Information
- About TED: www.ted.com/pages/about
- 25 TED talks perfect for classrooms: edudemic.com/2012/03/25-ted-talks-perfect-for-classrooms/
- With a new educational platform, TED gives teachers the keys to a flipped classroom: techcrunch.com/2012/04/24/ted-launches-new-ed-platform/
- TEDED: ed.ted.com

Final Two Apps—One for Fun and One Not

The only similarity between the two apps in this category is that they are both apps that have unique functions and they are both very appropriate for use by all educators. Despite those similarities, there is one major difference. The first is fun, and the second, quite frankly, is not. The second one is not designed to engage students, but its purpose is simply to provide teachers with a needed resource.

⟶≈≈⟵

Qrafter—QR Code Reader and Generator
Kerem Erakan
Website: www.facebook.com/Qrafter
Cost: Free for Reader; $2.99 for Generator

QR stands for quick response. Invented in 1994 by Toyota, the use of the QR codes remained primarily in the business industry until recent years. Now, educators everywhere are recognizing the varied and fun ways to incorporate the codes into school activities. One code can contain up to four thousand characters of information. That information could simply be a website address. However, they can also be used as business cards, with detailed information.

A very valuable use is to display them next to art or science projects to give viewers detailed information. The code could open up a voice of a student explaining his or her work. As a colleague at Lipscomb once said, "Pretty cool stuff!" The websites listed in this category give several examples of how the codes are being used in education. A favorite activity with QR codes is using them for a scavenger hunt. It is a fun activity to use at professional development workshops and also in student classrooms.

Qrafter was the first QR code app that was designed specifically for the iPad. The app can be downloaded for free. The reading function is free, but, if you read the fine print on iTunes, it mentions that it can generate QR codes only if the Pro Pack is purchased. However, if teachers want to avoid spending the money, there are also innumerable websites that generate these codes for free. An article below lists ten free online QR code generators. The second website below provides one of the best websites for generating codes.

Figure 3.6 shows the opening screen of Qrafter. Two icons at the bottom of the screen allow users to switch back and forth between reading an existing code (Scan) and generating a new one (Create). With the Scan icon highlighted, users are most likely to be using the Scan with Camera option. After tapping on the camera, users are given the option to toggle between the forward- and rear-facing cameras. The default is the rear-facing camera, which is used far more frequently.

Users simply hold the iPad up where the code is in the center of the four corners. A chime indicates that the image has been captured, and it then appears at the bottom of the screen. There are several other options, but the one most frequently used is the arrow icon, on the bottom right, which provides

Figure 3.6.   Qrafter app, ready to read QR code

seven options for sending or saving the icon. Figure 3.6 shows those seven options on the pop-up window that opens after tapping on the Send icon.

Teachers should check out all the sites below, but especially give attention to the first three links. The third link discusses how to use QR links for fun scavenger hunts. This is an activity that works well in all subject areas. Those hunts can effectively be used with teams for pretest reviews. Other websites provide other excellent ideas for classroom uses of QR codes.

Sampling of Websites with Qrafter Information
- Creating QR codes with Qrafter: www.youtube.com/watch?v=4-JUPfFVoJ8
- Recommended online QR code generator: www.qrstuff.com/
- iPad QR code scavenger hunt: www.youtube.com/watch?v=DrW3iXPmaiE
- Why you should start using QR codes in your classroom: edudemic.com/2012/09/start-qr-codes-classroom/
- QR codes—Prezi shows uses of QR codes in education: prezi.com/fgdhsvx1iyib/qr-codes/
- 10 ways to use QR codes in a history classroom (or any classroom): www.technologybitsbytesnibbles.info/archives/5348
- Top 10 free online QR code generators: freenuts.com/top-10-free-online-qr-code-generators/

—ᴄᴇᴇᴏ—

Common Core Standards
MasteryConnect
Website: www.masteryconnect.com/
Cost: Free; also available on Android

Although this poor little app has been designated as "not fun," that should not take away from the value that this app can offer to educators. Educators are well aware of the importance today of the Common Core. This app provides an easy way to access specific standards. The website below gives an excellent review of the app. When users open it, there are two sections: The Standards and More Resources. Each folder within the Standards section opens to folders with grade levels. The folder for each grade level contains all the specific standards. The Resources section has valuable information all educators can use.

One Website on Common Core Standards App
- Article and teacher review: www.edudemic.com/free-common-core-app-organizes-standards-by-grade-level/

Reflections on Chapter 3

Take a moment to reflect. Within chapters 2 and 3, descriptions have been provided for twenty-three of the very best apps for those who work in the field of education. Nearly two dozen is a meager number compared to the over one million apps that Apple has approved for use on the iPad (Brian, 2012). Each of these apps has risen to the top to be part of an illustrious group that has unique capabilities, which allow it to be delineated from the pack. Decisions for selecting these apps were made after both extensive readings and nearly three years of personal experience.

Readings included instructional sites, written by the creators of the apps, as well as various independent sources. Selections were based not purely on the readings but also on personal experiences and innumerable interviews with elementary, middle, and high school educators. Were there other apps that could be included? Absolutely! However, in the interest of conserving space, some excellent apps have not been included. Readers are encouraged to explore the "also ran" lists independently.

Several highly popular apps, such as iMovie, Twitter, Pinterest, Noteability, and VoiceThread, were considered for inclusion. Additionally, there are other apps, such as Dictionary and Google Earth, that rightly could have been included here. However, Google Earth is included in chapter 5, with other social studies apps, and Dictionary is in chapter 4, with language arts apps.

For those who are interested in keeping up with significant changes that relate to these apps, as well as learning about new apps that deserve recognition, I have created a private wiki. Directions for being a member of the wiki are provided in the introduction to this book.

Now, as a closing thought, use your QR code scanner to read the closing paragraph of this chapter, courtesy of Qrafter and the website qrstuff.com.

Figure 3.7.

CHAPTER FOUR

—⚘—

Teaching Language Arts
with the iPad

Introduction

Groucho Marx once said, "Outside of a dog, a book is man's best friend. Inside of a dog, it's too dark to read" (Sherrin, 2008). What would he say now that man has the iPad? Books remain important when it comes to teaching language arts, but many children and teachers consider the iPad not only a book but also a friend. There are innumerable apps that assist teachers in their instruction of reading and writing. This chapter includes fifteen of the very best: five each for elementary, middle, and high school.

Language Arts Apps for
Elementary School Students (K–4)

Word Wall HD (recommended grades: PK–K)
Punflay/Emantras, Inc.
Website: www.punflay.com
Cost: $1.99
Common Core Standards area: Foundational Skills

In January 2013, the *Parenting* website, listed below, recommended Word Wall HD as its App of the Week. This app offers both teachers and parents help in facilitating the learning of letters and word recognition. After a cute kitty jumps across a wall, the home screen comes up with links to six major areas. In Figure 4.1, an arrow has been added from each of those links, pointing to a sample image from the six areas.

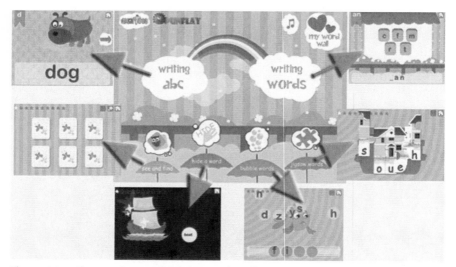

Figure 4.1. Six exercises available in Word Wall

In other words, tapping on "writing abc" brings up a screen full of letters; students can select any letter. Then a recording instructs students to drag and drop the letter over the same letter at the bottom of the screen. If the letter "d" is chosen, a recording sounds out the letter "d" immediately after it has been dropped into position. Then, as the image of a dog is shown, as seen in Figure 4.1, a recording states "D is for dog." On the home page, students might want to start by tapping on the musical note, at the top, which toggles through a selection of three background songs, with a fourth option to turn off the music.

Also, on the home page, tapping on the "writing words" cloud provides practice with two-letter combinations, each called a "word family." With two letters, students can practice saying the two letters, both alone and with another letter to spell a variety of words. In the See and Find area, either an easy or hard level of difficulty can be selected. Then, as a word or image appears, students try to match the corresponding word or image.

For the "hide a word" section, students can drag the little white circle around the area of the screen to find a word. Most of the screen is dark, but the circle serves as a flashlight. As soon as the word is discovered, an image of the word appears, as shown at the lower left of Figure 4.1. In "bubble words" students need to drag and drop the letters into their correct position to spell the word that corresponds to a picture. Then "jigsaw words" allows students to put the puzzle in place so that the word is spelled correctly.

Finally, in the "my word wall" section, students create a wall with the words and letters that they have learned. This area does not work well with shared iPads. For related information, the two websites below both relate to Word Wall HD:

- Parenting: www.parenting.com/blogs/children-and-technology-blog/ jeana-lee-tahnk/app-week-word-wall-hd
- Example of a child using Word Wall: www.youtube.com/watch?v=xw oeu9W3oeE

—⁓—

Abby—Animals Phonics Island Adventure (recommended grades: K–2)
22learn, LLC
Website: 22learn.com/app/6/phonics-island.html
Cost: Free or $1.99
Common Core Standards areas: Reading: Foundational Skills and Speaking and Listening

The free version of this app opens with a screen that has links for updating to the paid version, as well as for buying twelve other apps. The $1.99 version is well worth the extra fee, but using the free version first can be helpful in making a decision concerning an upgrade. Tapping on the sun graphic starts the app. On the Menu page, the information link is in the upper-left corner and the settings, on the top-right corner. The information includes the statement that "the application is designed to teach children initial word sounds as recommended by the Montessori method."

From that initial page, a tap on the sun brings out a cute little monkey, named Abby, who flies her airplane and lands on Phonics Island. Throughout the game, students can hear and repeat sounds. However, with the free version, only the letters S, M, T, and A are available. With the paid version, all the letters are available in seven groups. Within each grouping, students must complete six steps before being able to proceed to the next group of letters.

The cute monkey lands on the island, and explains that students are to be the drivers of a train. At the first stop, students match letters on cards, which allows a letter from each matched set to be placed on the train.

After successfully completing the task, students can pick a sticker to drag to a board. In the Settings menu, students can turn off this option for stickers. For the next five stops, students hear the sound that a specific letter makes. Students are then asked to drag an animal or animals that start with that sound to the train.

Figure 4.2. Level 1 of Animal Phonics Island Adventure

Figure 4.2 shows the fourth stop in the first group of letters. The stars at the top indicate how many stops have been successfully completed. Again, after each stop, students can pick another sticker for their boards. After completing level 1, in the paid version, students can then go to subsequent parts of the island and practice with a new grouping of letters. The background is different, but the game is played virtually the same way through all the letter groupings.

———◦◦◦———

Abby Pal Tracer—ABC Cursive HD (recommended grades: 2–4)
Hien Ton
Website: www.braincounts.com/BrainGames/AbbyPalTracer_ABCPrint.aspx
Cost: Free and $1.99
This app was designed by a group of teachers to give students a new way to practice cursive writing. Since Common Core does not have a standard related to cursive writing, many schools have opted to no longer teach this skill or to limit the classroom time for instruction and practice with this skill. This app has been selected in the hope that some schools are still using cursive writing and, if not, that parents will step up to fill the void.

When the app is opened, a friendly pencil, named Abby Pal, welcomes students and gives the direction to "Touch any letter to start." After a letter is tapped, Abby Pal moves off to the right, and dotted lines appear on the screen so the students can trace the letter. In Figure 4.3, there is also a graphic of a bird in the lower-right corner and the associated word in the left corner. Before tracing the letter, students can choose from a selection of eight colors on the lower right. Numbers are placed over the lines so students can follow them in order. If students do not trace them in the right order, the letter giggles, indicating an error.

Initially, only a portion of a letter is numbered. When students finish one section, then the next section is numbered. The options button on the right allows teachers to set line thickness and background music volume, as well as to select lowercase/uppercase, on/off sound effects, and on/off for the Startup Formal Introduction. That last option allows the friendly pencil to say a few extra words at the opening screen.

This app is particularly valuable for students who need practice with cursive writing. The friendly pencil makes encouraging remarks every time a letter is traced accurately.

Figure 4.3. Tracing the numbers

Note: The designer has created two other similar apps, Abby Pal Tracer—ABC Print HD and Abby Pal Tracer—Numbers HD.

————☙☙☙————

Cimo Can Spell (Lite) (recommended grades: K–3)
PlaySmart-Kids
Website: playsmart-kids.appspot.com/
Cost: Free or $2.99
Common Core Standards areas: Reading and Foundational Skills

Cimo Spelling Sight is an engaging app that helps children to recognize letter sounds and spell words correctly. The designer explains that with this app "[s]ome of the app's 100 words can be sounded out using common phonics rules (i.e., grouped by short vowel, long vowel, Bossy R's and other vowel team words, and others do not follow those normal rules and must be memorized." The penguin, Cimo, always wants to get across a span of cold water to retrieve a fish that is lying on the other side. In the short-vowel section, the speaker might ask a child to spell a word such as "zag." The child should drag and drop each letter into the correct position.

As a letter is moved the recording says the name of the letter. If the letters are put in the correct position, little Cimo slowly moves across each letter, as the recording again says the name of each letter. When the fish is retrieved, the word is shown on the screen. On the left side of Figure 4.4, the word is spelled correctly, so Cimo is able to retrieve and eat the fish.

When words are spelled correctly, a recording first repeats the word, then repeats each letter sound again, and finally says the word again. If a child misspells any of the words, the penguin falls into the water, as shown on the right side of Figure 4.4, and the recording says, "Let's try again!" After two

Figure 4.4.   On the left, a child spells "zag" correctly; on the right, another child spells it incorrectly.

attempts with an incorrect spelling, the recording gives the correct spelling. Level 1, Short Vowels has twelve words. This app provides the following six levels:

1. Vowels
2. Long vowels
3. Bossy R's
4. Other vowel teams
5. Irregular vowels
6. Challenge level

For any single game, students are asked to spell twelve words. By tapping on the Report & Setup button, teachers can see a record with the number of times a word was asked and the percentage of times that a correct answer was given. Each of the six levels has a set of words, from which twelve can be selected. At the top right of the Report screen is a Setup button. By tapping there, teachers or parents have several options, including the ability to change the number of questions within each game, as well as constraints for the level of difficulty.

Altogether the designer offers four Cimo apps. Another free app is Cimo Spelling Site, which provides fifty of the most commonly used words. Upgrades for each of the free apps cost $2.99 but include 255 words. Each Cimo app is a delightful and definitely useful tool to assist with the mission of teaching spelling at the elementary level.

——✦——

Booksy: Learn to Read Platform for K–2 (recommended grades: K–3)
Tipitap, Inc.
Website: www.tipitap.com
Cost: Free for three books; additional books $0.99 each; also available on Android
Common Core Standards areas: Reading Literature, Reading: Informational Text

At the website 20 iPad Apps to Teach Elementary Reading, listed below, and on many other related sites, Booksy is highly recommended. Each book included with this app has the following impressive features:

1. Tapping on any individual word that seems difficult to readers elicits a recording of the correct pronunciation.

2. Each book has an associated quiz that tests for reading comprehension.
3. Records are saved of each book that has been read, whether completed or only partially read.
4. Students can receive achievement awards for completing books, for reading at least one book every day, and for performing well on quizzes. Students always appreciate getting awards for their efforts. Reports can be emailed to parents or teachers.
5. Recordings are made as students read books. The settings area allows those recordings and a general progress report to be sent by email to teachers, parents, or grandparents. (While students' voices are being recorded, a red button is lit at the bottom left of a book's page.)
6. The free Humpback Whales book includes fascinating information, including about 30 seconds of a male's "love song."

Despite those wonderful features, only three books come with the free version. Regardless, at the current time, this app currently trumps all the others in the category of teaching reading to early elementary students. A few extra books for $0.99 each are well worth the investment. Occasionally, sets of ten books have been offered for $4.99. Each book comes with the same features as described above.

The first time the app is used, the opening screen comes up with an overlay that explains about the different features available from that home page. The overlay can be deleted and will not appear again unless users tap on the Help button, on the bottom right. Teachers or parents can start by tapping on the Parental Dashboard, on the lower left. Figure 4.5 shows the various settings that can be made. Tapping on the blue ribbon on the top right brings up a page that shows the various student awards, as mentioned in the fourth feature above.

At the bottom, the My Reading Log section shows the number of times that the various books were read. Back on the Parental Dashboard, tapping on the graphic of any book brings up a screen that shows the statistics associated with the usage of the book (how many times read, quiz scores, etc.). Recordings that were made of students' reading the books are also available on that window.

This is a remarkable and worthy app. On each page of the various books, a single-finger scroll up shows a menu, at the bottom of the screen, that provides additional features. The left area provides a scrollbar to control brightness, a red Recording button that lights up whenever students are reading, and a button to begin the recorded professional reading of the text. On the

Figure 4.5.   Parental Dashboard

right of the lower menu, students can quickly scroll through the pages to any specific page.

Note: Booksy: School Edition is available for $9.99, which is designed for school purchases.

Related website—20 iPad apps to teach elementary reading: www.teach thought.com/

Apps-2/20-ipad-apps-to-teach-elementary-reading/

Applications to other subjects: This also has value for science classes. In addition to the Humpback Whale, several of the 99-cent books are appropriate for teaching science to young children. Children love learning the sounds that animals make! In addition, many of the books can be purchased in Spanish.

Additional Highly Rated Apps
My Story—Book Maker for Kids
HiDef Web Solution
Website: mystoryapp.org/
Cost: Free

This app provides an excellent way to introduce young children to the thrill of creating their own books. The app allows for artistic creations. As a free and highly rated app, it arguably deserves more than this meager mention.

Language Arts Apps for Middle School Students (5–8)

Dictionary.com Dictionary & Thesaurus for iPad (recommended grades: 5–12)
Dictionary.com, LLC
Website: dictionary.reference.com/
Cost: Free, $0.99, or $4.99; also available on Android
Common Core Standards areas: Reading Literature, Language

Dictionaries have always had an essential role in language arts classrooms. However, because of the evolution of so many digital technologies, this dictionary app has far more to offer than its hard-copy counterpart. The home screen provides a Word of the Day, as well as links to slideshows, articles, and websites that have relevance to the power of vocabulary. Most students use this app by simply typing a word into the search box, at the top of the screen. Students who are unsure of the spelling of a word can tap on the little microphone, which is just to the right of the search box, to speak the word.

If the correct pronunciation is used, the definition readily appears. If the word is mispronounced, students receive either a message that no word was found or a list of possible words that sound similar. Unfortunately, the free app allows only five free voice-to-text searches. One hundred additional searches can be purchased for $0.99.

When a word is found, three icons are provided on the upper-right side of the screen. Tapping on the star saves the word to a list of favorite words. Students can tap on the arrow to email the word to themselves or perhaps a teacher. The word can also be sent to Facebook and Twitter. Tapping on the icon between the star and send graphic sends students to a translation area, where sentences or paragraphs can be translated to nearly thirty languages.

In the upper-left corner is a link to the menu, which brings up the listing shown in Figure 4.6. The Thesaurus button will simply change the menu bar

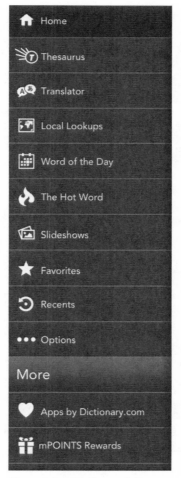

Figure 4.6. Dictionary left menu

to yellow, but when a search is done, a list of both synonyms and antonyms is provided. The next five links all provide valuable areas that classroom teachers can use for instructional purposes.

Finally, tapping on the Options link simply brings up a screen that is mostly about upgrades. The Power Pack upgrade adds example sentences and rhyming, medical, and science dictionaries, for a single price, currently set at $7.99. The other upgrades are listed below with the current price:

- Example sentences: $1.99
- Rhyming dictionary: $1.99
- Medical dictionary: $2.99
- Science dictionary: $2.99
- Remove ads: $4.99
- Voice credits: $0.99 for one hundred more voice searches
- Translator: $1.99 for one translator

At the bottom of the list of upgrades are four additional areas:

- Rate this app
- Share this app
- Feedback to the designer
- About Dictionary.com

This app obviously has features that make it far more valuable than the dusty dictionary on the shelf that students rarely use. Students enjoy this way of finding information, which allows them to increase their vocabulary.

—◦◦◦—

Free Books—23,469 classics to go (recommended grades: 7–12)
Digital Press Publishing
Website: spreadsong.com/
Cost: Free, $0.99, or $3.99; also available on Android
Common Core Standards areas: Reading Literature, Reading: Informational Text

Did that say "Free"? Indeed, it did! The typical free reading app comes with only two or three free books. However, this app comes with thousands of classics available to read, although with only a few additional features. The primary advantages for upgrading to the $3.99 version are eliminating the commercials and adding 4,727 audiobooks.

The top of the home screen has over five dozen scrollable images, in alphabetical order, which represent both authors and subject areas. Figure 4.7 shows that Mark Twain has been selected. Jules Verne, Voltaire, and H. G. Wells are other authors showing, as well as two subject areas, War and Western. Selecting an author provides several paragraphs about the author, as well as a selection of the author's most famous quotes. Within subject areas, a couple of paragraphs describe the available literature that relates to that subject. Tapping on a specific work brings up a window with more information and links to initiate a download.

Also, as shown in Figure 4.7, the right area has a scrollable list of all the available books by the author or in a specific subject area. Tabs are available at the top of that area so that the list can be in order of titles, authors, most popular, or highest ratings. When a book is selected, a new window comes up with a description of the book and associated ratings. A green Download and Read button allows the book to be placed on the app's bookcase page.

In the Library area, as shown in Figure 4.7, tapping on the tab on the Browse tab opens a new window that has a bookcase, with all the available books that have been downloaded. Users can tap on any book to open and

Figure 4.7. Library window of Free Books

read it. While reading books, students can tap on the star at the top to rate them. Adjustments can be made for the letter size, as well as the brightness, color theme, and layout.

Finally, this app has recently added a Dropbox integration feature that allows users to import other eBooks that have been saved to their Dropbox accounts. An Import from Dropbox button, on the upper left of the Browse area, allows users to start that process.

Applications to other subjects: Because several subjects are listed in the library area, this app can also be used in social studies classes. Three related topics that are listed are history, politics, and war.

—⬥⬥⬥—

My Grammar Lab Intermediate (recommended grades: 7–12)
Pearson Education
Website: www.pearsonk12.com/
Cost: Free; also available on Android
Common Core Standards area: Language

Without any particular glitz, this app is replete with hundreds of practice grammar questions, as well as definitions of grammar terminology. The app is designed for use with the Pearson book *MyGrammar Lab Intermediate B1/B2* (Mark Foley & Diane Hall, 2012). Without the textbook, no explanations are provided for errors. Regardless, there are ample practice problems, as well as a large glossary.

The home page offers only those two options, Practice or Glossary. The Glossary brings up a list, in alphabetical order, of all grammar terms (action verb, active, adjective, adverb, etc.). Tapping on any one of those terms gives a short definition. Tapping on the practice button brings up a list of twenty modules, each with four or more units, for a total of 110 units.

Each unit practice test provides a selection of ten, twenty, twenty-five, or thirty questions. With a correct answer, a small window will pop up with a Correct message. With an incorrect answer, the window that pops up has the specific unit in the Pearson book to look in to find the correct information. That window can also be accessed by tapping on the lightbulb icon that is below each question.

If students wish to study more first, a little "skip" button is provided at the top right. Information is always provided at the end of a quiz, showing the number of correct and incorrect answers, as well as the percentage score. Pure and simple, this app was developed to work together with the afore-mentioned textbook. However, even without the text, the beauty of the app is that it offers additional practice for students who want to improve their knowledge about English grammar.

—⁓—

Maxjournal (recommended grades: 7–12)
Omaxmedia
Website: omaxmedia.com
Cost: Free
Common Core Standards areas: Writing, Language

Journaling is an important part of the middle school experience, and iTunes offers plenty of journaling apps. This app is not the highest-rated app overall, but it is the highest-rated choice from all education-related journal apps. In the introductory section, the designers include the statement, "Our philosophy in designing this software is to keep it simple, intuitive and straightforward." That is perfect for middle school students!

The opening screen simply has an area to tap to start a new journal. Two choices are provided: Create a New Blank Journal or Create a Journal from a Maxjournal Backup file. The second choice is for backups that students previously saved, so for new users the blank journal should be the selection. The next screen to come up is the Journal Wizard. Students should type in a journal title, such as "Johnny T.'s Seventh Grade Journal." Pictures can be selected for the journal cover, and then there are four choices for the background. As journals are created, they become viewable on the home page.

Before the students write in their journals, teachers need to explain some of the basic features. Only three icons are available on the top menu bar of the home screen. The plus icon starts a new journal. The middle icon can adjust the background, and the question mark opens a selection of various areas to assist with the app. As a journal is opened, there are six icons in the upper-right corner that are a bit hard to see, but they each serve an important function, as indicated below:

- The first icon represents a calendar. Tapping there opens the calendar page. Each day on the calendar has the beginning text of the journal entry that was made on that day. By double tapping on any specific day, viewers can read the full entry for that day. Tapping on the Today button, on the top right, brings viewers back to the current journal page.
- The second icon opens a window in which students can email their journals to teachers. After selecting the date range for the file, a choice can be made for sending the file as Simple Text or a PDF. After tapping

on Email, an email window pops up. The address can be added and a message included. Then the Exported journal will be sent on its way.

- The magnifying glass is the third icon in the menu bar. That initiates a search, which can be done by specific text, tags, ratings, or time.
- The fourth icon looks like an eye; it allows for quick changes in the background colors.
- The fifth icon, two As, allows changes in the journal page's font, letter size, and text brightness. The text background can be adjusted from black text on white to white text on black.
- The sixth icon, the question mark, brings up a new window that provides thirteen topics, which gives more information about the workings of Maxjournal. Finally images can be attached to any journal page. Images can be inserted from any Album in the Photo area of the iPad.

This is just another one of those apps that allow for a paperless classroom. Teachers love receiving journals through email.

—⁓—

Subtext (recommended grades: 7–12)
Subtext
Website: www.subtext.com/
Cost: Free
Common Core Standards areas: Writing, Language, Speaking and Listening (7.SL.1)

This last app for middle school classrooms was selected to be sure that all areas of the Common Core were covered. Speaking and Listening is the one remaining area not addressed by the previous four apps. This clearly can be done through Skype, but that app was already covered in chapter 3. The first evidence, under Speaking and Listening, is to have students "Engage effectively in a range of collaborative discussions."

For the vast majority of middle school students, engaging in collaborative discussions is an entirely new experience. Subtext is an excellent app for giving students an initial understanding of the meaning of collaborative discussions. First developed in 2012, this innovative app may seem complex initially, but there are plenty of help areas. The designers give the following description of this app:

TURN ANY BOOK OR DOCUMENT INTO A DIGITAL CLASSROOM—
In Subtext teachers and students can exchange ideas as they read, right in the pages of nearly any digital book or document. You can also layer in enrichment

materials, assignments and quizzes opening up limitless opportunities to engage students, foster analysis and writing skills, and assess student progress. Subtext's service extends the reading experience far beyond traditional books and aligns with the Common Core Standards across reading, writing and 21st century digital skills. (download.cnet.com/Subtext/3000-20415_4-75604779.html)

In the opening screen, users can sign in with either Edmodo or Google/Gmail and then select the role of teacher, student, or parent. The next window brings up a screen that provides overlays to explain the various areas. The Welcome to Subtext for Teachers booklet, near the top, is an important area, explaining that Subtext allows teachers to do the following activities:

- Create a group
- Find content
- Highlight and tag key concepts
- Add a discussion
- Embed a link or image
- Take instruction further

On the left, there is a button with instructions to Tap to Add Books & Articles. In the pop-up window, four choices are provided:

1. Find free and paid books that can be typed into a search area
2. Find free web articles to read within Subtext
3. Find featured books and articles by grade level
4. Browse your public library

In the grade level area, Top Free Books for Middle School Levels, for example, brings up twenty-four well-known books. Each book is rated and has associated information. *The Story of My Life*, by Helen Keller, can be selected for both My Shelf and the Group Shelf. A group needs to be created before users can add books there. Another important area is Common Core Books, separated by grade level. As books are selected, they show up at the top of the screen, along with the three books that were provided by default. As more books are loaded, users can scroll through all the books.

Creating a group is a straightforward process. In the lower right Group area, users can tap on the plus sign and then type in a the title of a group. Immediately, a message appears that the Group Code has been emailed to the user. Each group has a unique code that must be distributed to the students who are to be part of that group. The emails arrive quickly and contain associated directions. Below are three websites that are very useful for new users of this app:

- Blog with discussions about getting started with Subtext: kulowiectech .blogspot.com/2012/05/social-reading-on-ipad-subtext-x-custom.html
- Support page from designers of the app: www.subtext.com/support
- Suggestions for using Subtext with book discussions: www.freetech4 teachers.com/2012/06/subtext-great-app-for-book-discussions.html# .UTDaUxkq9BE

Language Arts Apps for High School Students (Grades 9–12)

English Grammar (recommended grades: 9–12)
blufish, LLC
Website: tmoana.wix.com/blufish#!universal-apps
Cost: $1.99
Common Core Standards area: Language

Many students consider grammar to be bland and boring. However, its importance cannot be overstated not only for success in school but also for employability. By using good grammar, students have the assurance that what they write and speak can be clearly understood. Despite the lack of any interactive features, this app provides an excellent resource for either whole-class or individual use.

The entire app is quite simply a 284-page textbook. In the preface, the author explains that he designed the book to be "simple, direct and dignified," covering the basics of grammar and composition, "deal[ing] particularly with the sources of frequent error . . . and omit[ting] the non-essential." He also states that the book "contain[s] an abundance of exercises and practical work."

From anywhere in the book, the table of contents, shown in Figure 4.8, can be accessed from a button, in the lower left. In each of the twelve chapters, the author provides numbered lists of important points, followed by a good number of related exercises. Throughout the twelve chapters, there are a total of 284 pages, with 226 key points and 86 exercises. However, within each of those categories there is a considerable amount of information. At only $1.99, this book is a bargain!

Chapter 7 is typical of all the chapters. For the topic of sentences, only eight grammar rules are covered; each is explained succinctly with a couple of related examples. Then a collection of related exercises follows. The chapter includes eight exercises, each with a large selection of questions;

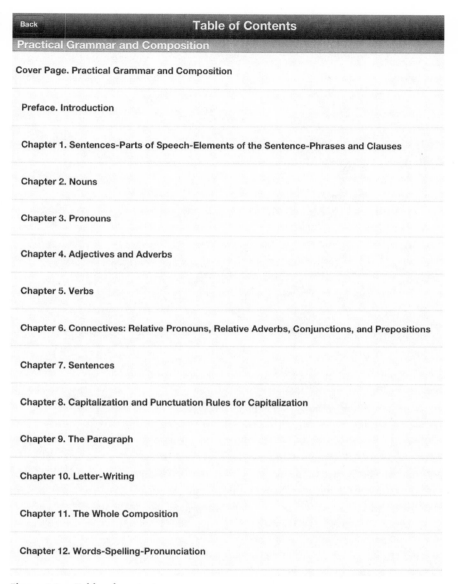

Figure 4.8.   Table of contents

altogether the chapter includes over two hundred questions. Exercise sixty-six asks students to combine each of seventeen groups of sentences into "one well constructed long sentence."

The last group includes the following sentences: "The pleasantest month is June. It has flowers. It has mild weather. It has a slight haze in the atmosphere.

These things seem to flood one's soul with peace and contentment." Obviously, there is not a single correct answer. Students could work on this exercise in groups and then decide on a best answer. The exercises are truly the essence of this app. Teachers can use them for full class discussions but then can equally well assign specific ones for classwork or homework.

Vocabulary for GRE, SAT, ACT, GMAT, IELTS, TOEFL, and ESL (recommended grades: 6–12)
SuVoBi
Website: suvobi.com/
Cost: Free initially; other options $0.99 or $6.99
Common Core Standards area: Language

Amid a plethora of vocabulary apps on iTunes, this one is the only five-star vocabulary app available. The opening screen, as shown on the left side of Figure 4.9, provides links to six areas. The Help section has about three screens full of information. The Select Skin section provides nine selections for the background.

The Select Vocab Lists brings up a marvelous selection of eight lists of increasing difficulty, as shown on the right side of Figure 4.9. For high school users, the SAT and Academic Word List are probably the most appropriate. Users may select as many items from the lists as they wish. Interestingly, ACT is not included in the vocabulary list, although it is listed in the title.

The only yellow background button, on the home screen, Learn provides learners with the opportunity to become familiar with new words. This app has an approach different from so many other vocabulary apps, which function simply like virtual flash cards. With this app, users are provided with a new word and the associated definition so they can study the word first. When the drill begins, students see the definition of a word. Six words are listed below the definition, each with a button to hear the correct pronunciation.

If students select the words that correctly match the definitions, a green check mark briefly appears, and then the drill continues to a new definition. However, if students select the wrong word, a screen comes up that shows the correct answer. They can then take time to study the word. If students are unsure of the word, they can simply tap on the "i" button, which provides the correct answer.

The Unlock Credits section provides an indication of how many words have been learned. Learning a word is determined by multiple correct answers on the drills. Once the app has determined that a word was "learned," students are awarded a point. After sixty points are earned, more points will

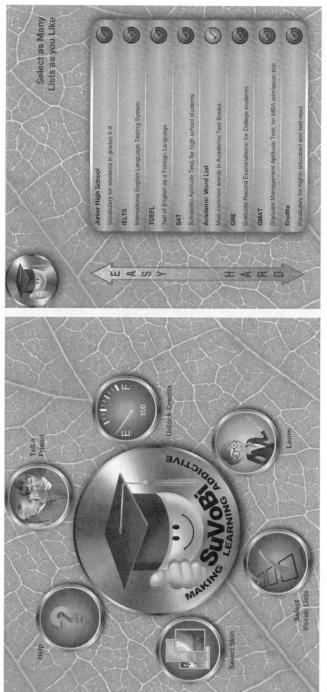

Figure 4.9. Home screen on the left and eight vocabulary lists on the right

need to be purchased to continue with the program. For example, one hundred credits can be purchased for $0.99, or unlimited points can be acquired for $6.99. It takes some time to acquire the sixty or one hundred points, but still, if the funds are available, the $6.99 option might be the best for long-term use.

Applications to other subjects: Two of the tests provided with this app, TOEFL and IELTS, have obvious applications to ELL/ESL classrooms. ELL apps are covered in chapter 6 of the second book in this set.

—⁓—

SwipeSpeare—Modern Shakespeare (recommended grades: 9–12)
Book Caps
Website: www.swipespeare.com
Cost: Free
Common Core Standards area: Reading Literature (both *Macbeth* and *Hamlet* are included as Text Exemplars for Drama)

If Shakespeare could come back to visit us today, he would surely be impressed with the extensive collection of Shakespeare apps. Unfortunately, most of the high-quality apps are also high cost. This free app seems to be a remarkable exception. The only catch is that only a portion of the app is free. Some additional fees are required to obtain the full texts of all Shakespeare's work. Specifics are explained below. Regardless, SwipeSpeare still stood out as one of the most highly rated Shakespearean apps.

One of the popular features of this app is its ability to switch between an actual text and the modern English version. Students appreciate another feature that allows them to tap and hold on any unfamiliar word to bring up the word's definition. The opening screen offers eleven categories, the first of which is a biography of Shakespeare. That biography includes four sections:

- The times Shakespeare lived in
- Shakespeare's family
- Shakespeare's childhood and education
- Shakespeare's adulthood

The initial three categories contain three to four screens' worth of information. However, Shakespeare's adulthood contains more extensive information, from the time Shakespeare was twenty-one years old until his death. The next four categories on the opening screen link to areas where specific works can be accessed:

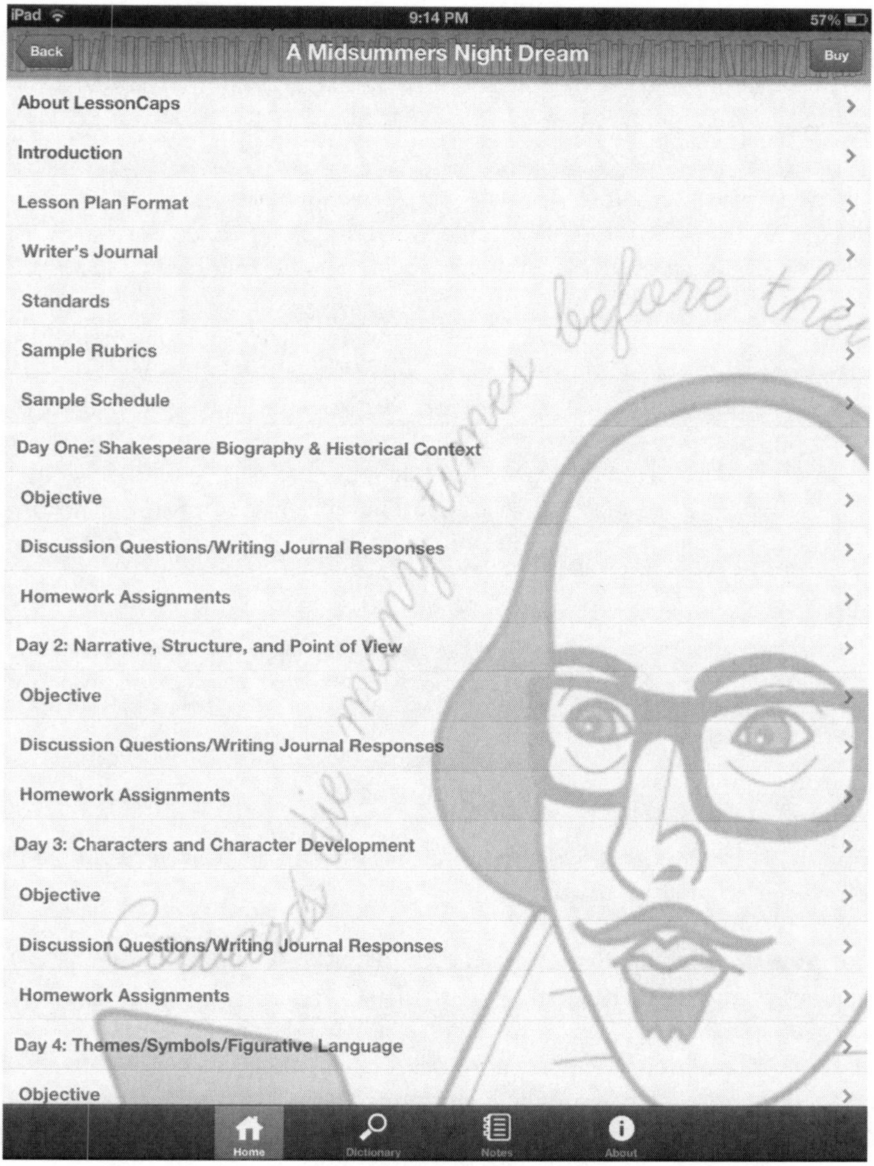
iPad
9:14 PM
57%
Back
A Midsummers Night Dream
Buy
About LessonCaps
Introduction
Lesson Plan Format
Writer's Journal
Standards
Sample Rubrics
Sample Schedule
Day One: Shakespeare Biography & Historical Context
Objective
Discussion Questions/Writing Journal Responses
Homework Assignments
Day 2: Narrative, Structure, and Point of View
Objective
Discussion Questions/Writing Journal Responses
Homework Assignments
Day 3: Characters and Character Development
Objective
Discussion Questions/Writing Journal Responses
Homework Assignments
Day 4: Themes/Symbols/Figurative Language
Objective
Home
Dictionary
Notes
About

Figure 4.10. Index for *A Midsummer Night's Dream*

- Comedy plays (16)
- History plays (10)
- Tragedy plays (12)
- Sonnets (154).

The Bard is accredited with writing thirty-eight plays and 154 sonnets, and every work of Shakespeare is represented in this app. Every act and every scene of *Romeo and Juliet* is viewable within this free app. However, for the other fifty-seven plays, only the first act is included for free, with the full version available for $1.99. Thirty-one sonnets are fully included with the free app, and the remaining 123 are viewable for a $1.99 charge. There are discounted prices for buying all the plays within a category, as well as a price for buying all of the Bard's works.

The best features of this app are the teacher lesson plans and study guides, accessible by tapping on Teacher Lesson Plans, from the home page. Figure 4.10 shows the index for the Lesson Plans associated with A *Midsummer Night's Dream.*

All the information through Sample Rubrics is included free with the app. The remaining material, which includes five days' worth of material, is again available for a fee. The study guides are likewise partly free and partly for purchase.

⟶⟵

Constitution and Federalist Papers (recommended grades: 9–12)
Multieducator, Inc.
Website: www.multieducator.net/
Cost: Free
Common Core Standards area: Reading: Bill of Rights listed as Informational
    Text: English Language Arts (Grade 11-CCR)
Awesome! This app not only provides every word from the U.S. Constitution, but related documents are also included, such as the Federalist Papers, all twenty-seven amendments, and more. Yes, there is indeed more! This app provides an explanation with every article of every section of the Constitution, as well as with every amendment and all other included papers. That is great for a history class, but what is the U.S. Constitution doing in the language arts chapter?

For an answer to that question, read the Language Arts Standards of the Common Core (CCSS.ELA-Literacy.RI.11-12.9), which specify that students should be able to "analyze . . . U.S. documents of historical and literary significance (including . . . the Preamble to the Constitution, the Bill of

Figure 4.11. U.S. Constitution and Federalist Papers

Rights)." The menu associated with this app provides links to fourteen areas. As shown in Figure 4.11, those areas are:

- Background (with information about the app and about "The Writing of the Constitution")
- The Preamble
- Seven articles of the Constitution (each with one to ten sublinks to the various sections)
- The twenty-seven amendments
- the Madison Journals (about eighty journals, from May 14 to September 14, 1787)
- Federalist Papers (eighty-five in all)
- The Virginia Ratifying Convention (ten documents written in June 1788)
- The images of the Constitution (four images, which combine to show the complete document of the U.S. Constitution)

This is a valuable app for any high school English or social studies classroom. English teachers can use it to discuss and analyze the text. The app also comes with a dictionary that allows users to tap a word to find the definition.

Application to other subjects: This app is also perfect for all U.S. history and government classrooms!

———⁓———

iDeas for Writing (recommended grades: 10–12)
SCVisuais/Literautas
Website: www.literautas.com/en/apps/ideas-for-writing
Cost: $1.99
Common Core Standards area: Writing

On the website home page for this app, provided above, the developers begin their explanation of the features with the phrase "If you like to write . . ." The app was developed to assist fledging professional writers, although teachers will find it to be very effective for inspiring their students to develop better writing skills. iDeas offers ideas for getting started with the all-important first lines of any written work. Even more important for the novice writer at the high school level, there is a large area of writing exercises.

At the bottom of the home screen are Writing Tips. Users can swipe left on that area to bring up one of fifteen expressions of advice. One of the early inspirational statements says that one should "[w]rite every day between 100 and 500 words at least. After a year, you'll see how much you've improved."

A student who follows that advice is likely be able to meet all the Common Core Standards within the Writing section.

The home screen bears the title Creative Trigger, with links to four other main areas of the apps: First Lines, Title, Character, and Five Words. Tapping on First Lines shows a suggested first line for a creative work. Tapping on New, at the bottom, allows viewers to see a large collection of other first lines.

When a first line is found that seems to be appropriate, there is a Save button, which saves a selected sentence to the Saved area of the app. Teachers can allow students to make their own selections or assign a specific first line either to the whole class or to individual students. The remaining three links on the home screen work similarly. Returning to the Creative Trigger page can always be done by tapping on the ideas icon, at the bottom of the screen.

Figure 4.12 shows the Writing Exercises area of this app. This area is viewable by tapping on the Workshop icon, on the bottom menu. The star icon represents the Saved area and contains all the items that are saved, as mentioned in the previous paragraph. The Notebook icon links to an area where students can begin to do their writing. Finally, the Information area provides three main areas: Application features, Free writing resources, and Information about us.

The Application features page provides specific information about the app and how to use it, including two videos. The resources page provides information and links to ten articles about various aspects of writing. The Information about us page provides several paragraphs about the designers and their mission.

The six areas within the Writing Exercises page are where one of the two most important areas of this app is found. Each area then provides ten to nineteen sets of exercises, ranging in difficulty from low to medium to high. Teachers can assign areas, according to the talents of their students. The Notebook area is the second most important area of this app, perhaps even the most important area. All the actual writings are done in this area. Those writings can then be shared with teachers, family, or friends through email or Facebook.

App Appropriate for the English Classroom, but Described Elsewhere
PrepZilla Study with Friends Game
gWhiz, LLC
Cost: Free

This app is discussed in chapter 2 of *The Deuce and a Half iPad*. Topics include AP English language, AP English literature (McGraw-Hill), and AP English literature (FLVS).

Figure 4.12. Writing exercises

Reflections on Chapter 4

This chapter reflects the first of nine chapters, within this two-book set, that cover apps specific to one area of study. Some teachers have limited themselves to apps that can be applied only to all subject areas. That is a tragic restriction. Each one of the apps in this chapter and all other subject-specific chapters provides superior tools for enhancing the learning experience for students.

For young children, the ability to hear repeated letters and syllables pronounced in the Abby—Animals Phonics Island Adventure and Spelling with Cimo apps provides a superior learning experience. Reading can be greatly enhanced across all grade levels with the apps Booksy, Free Books, Subtext, and SwipeSpeare. Then Maxjournal and iDeas for Writing both offer students an intriguing way to acquire better writing skills.

Each of the apps in this chapter offers students ways to succeed in the use of the English language. The importance of that mission cannot be overstated for success in academia, the workplace, and social environments. New subject-specific apps are being designed all the time. As one of those new apps hits the market and rises to the top of its field, information will be added to the private wiki that was mentioned in the introduction to this book.

—◦◦◦—

CHAPTER FIVE

Teaching Social Studies with the iPad

Introduction

Concerning the study of history, a regrettable tradition was in place as far back as the Middle Ages. That is, in history class, students were required to memorize endless lists of dates and names. Interspersed amid bland and boring days of lecture were the terrifying classes when tests were administered. Recalling lists of, for example, all the kings of all the Greek city-states must have been just as insufferable to middle-age children as it is to children of today's classes.

Conscientious students might stay up late into the early morning hours, trying to memorize the names and dates, and yet still fail the test. Sadly, that exact scenario has been documented in innumerable schools, but it is not how history should be taught. Learning is not achieved through memorization.

Attempting to teach history through memorization succeeds only in instilling in most students a hatred of the subject. Teachers should make history "real" with vivid imagery of historic events. English philosopher and historian R. G. Collingwood once said, "Nothing capable of being memorized is history" (as cited in Bauer, 2003, p. 181). All history teachers need to forget memorization and bring out the iPads! Hands-on activities with the iPad can bring history to life. The apps in this chapter provide students with a fun way to gain understanding of major historical events and trends. And, yes, they will also learn some names and dates in the process.

Social Studies Apps for
Elementary School Students (K–4)

GeoMaster Plus (recommended grades: K–4)
Visuamobile
Website: www.geomasterapp.com/
Cost: Free in the United States; $3.99 for GeoMaster Plus HD (for all continents)

This app focuses on the United States, providing an excellent way for a young student to learn the names and locations of the states. Most of the other apps that do this require a fee. The opening screen for this app includes an appeal to upgrade to a full version, which includes maps for other countries and world capitals. To start this app, users can tap on the US States button. It may take a couple of seconds for a map to appear on the screen.

This app challenges students to correctly identify all fifty states, in as short a time as possible. After the name of a state appears, it then glides to the position at the top of the screen, along with the name of the state's capital. As students continue to tap on the states, the percentage of the fifty states that have been accurately selected shows in the lower-right corner. The running time is recorded in the upper-right corner.

When a user taps on an incorrect state, that state briefly is colored in red, and the name of that state appears, as shown in Figure 5.1. At the same time, the correct state is colored blue, with a circle showing where students should have tapped. For example, Figure 5.1 shows that the user incorrectly tapped West Virginia rather than Maryland. Those colors and the state name show only briefly. Any state that is not correctly answered remains in the pool of states, to pop up again later, until students select the correct answer.

After all the states have been selected, some clapping is heard, and the word "Bravo" appears on top of the map. That is followed by a window with the score, which is the time that users took to complete the activity. That score can be shared by email, Twitter, or Facebook. On the top left corner, the fraction shows the number of states correctly selected, over the number of attempts students made during the process of the game. By playing multiple times, students can continually try to decrease the amount of time taken to identify states.

This is an excellent game to play, both in the classroom and at home. With a small number of computers, each group could be given an iPad, which they would continually pass from student to student until all states were accurately identified. The winning group would be the one to complete the activity in the shortest time.

Figure 5.1. Incorrect selection shown in the circle

—⟨∿⟩—

Stack the States Lite (recommended grades: 2–4)
Dan Russell-Pinson
Website: dan-russell-pinson.com/my-games/
Cost: Free or $0.99; also available on Android

This game not only focuses on the location of states, but it also includes questions about state flags, state capitals, and national landmarks. For that reason, this app might be more appropriate for use with upper-elementary students. There are four links on the opening screen: Play Game, My States, Select Player, Get full version. The Select Player area allows up to six players, plus an additional guest. By tapping on a Player bar, students can add their names and choose a favorite state. After adding the names, the directions are provided.

As the game starts, a question appears at the top of the page, such as "Wyoming touches which state?" Below the graphic are names of four states, for example, Nebraska, Rhode Island, Kansas, and Oklahoma. If Nebraska is selected as one of the states to border Wyoming, students are able to move, rotate, and drop the state. If students answer incorrectly with any of the other states, the correct answer is revealed, but a new question appears, without allowing students to stack the state with any other states that were correctly answered.

The goal is to stack the states high enough to pass the bar, as shown in Figure 5.2. One of the fun events that might occur is that, even though questions are answered correctly, the stack of states may collapse if they are

Figure 5.2.   States successfully stacked to reach the bar

not properly balanced. When the states stay stable and pass the bar, there is a bit of fanfare, including music and a congratulatory message. In addition, students are told that they have earned a state. Tapping on the My States button on the home page accesses a map with those earned states.

The upgrade for this app is only $0.99 and includes a very valuable Learn area, which has fifty flash cards, each with information on the state's capital, flag, nickname, bordering states, major cities, and landmarks. Studying this area can help students to gain a higher level of accuracy with the games. There is also a question mark, at the lower left on the home screen, that allows users to vary the type of questions that are asked in that area.

—⁓—

Early Jamestown (recommended grades: 3–9)
Victory Productions
Website: www.victoryprd.com/
Cost: Free

This app focuses on early American history, with information that covers the time period from 1606 to 1780. Altogether, there are thirty-four "pages" of information, replete with images, videos, charts, and interactive maps. The home page welcomes users with instructions, as shown on Figure 5.3.

The top menu bar provides links to two ways of navigating around this app. Tapping on the top left of every page provides a link to the menu bar, which lists all pages with the dates and the title of the time period. On the right is a link to an area where viewers can scroll through miniature images of all the pages in the app to quickly select a familiar page.

The entire app functions like an interactive iBook, with only two chapters included. Chapter 3, titled "Strangers on the Shores," covers the birth of the Virginia Colony, with information from the preparations in England in the 1570s through the early years, up to 1700. Chapter 4, titled "A Growing Virginia," follows the previous chapter with some overlapping years, covering events from 1619–1750. In a typical page from this app, the lower-left area provides one of the many videos that are included with this app; those videos were created by the Jamestown–Yorktown Foundation in Williamsburg, Virginia.

Throughout the text, key words are colored to indicate a link. For example, when students tap on the indentured servants link, a Words to Know window pops up with the pronunciation and definition of the phrase. At the end of both chapters are two unique pages. First, there is a time line, with a summary of the key events that were covered in the chapter. The time line also has links that take viewers back to specific pages.

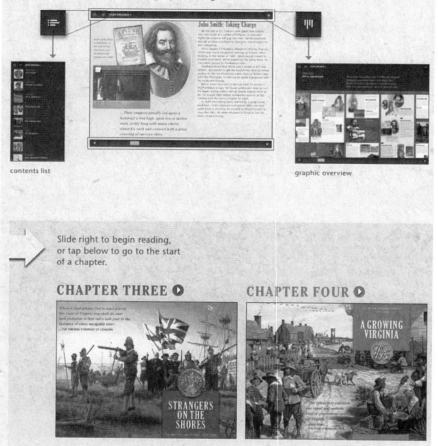

Figure 5.3. Home page

The last page in each chapter is a Let's Review page. There are several questions, with links back to the pages, that help viewers answer the questions. The Key Words are also listed there, as well as a Think and Do section. That last section provides excellent classroom activities that can make history come alive for the students. Early Jamestown is a quality app, and, considering the cost, this is a must-have app for all teachers who are teaching about this time period.

——ᴡᴡ——

ABE App (recommended grades: 3–6)
Eda-Soft
Website: www.eda-soft.com/Mobile/Home.html
Cost: Free; also available on Android

Without a shred of glitz, this app provides a fun way for elementary-level students to learn facts about arguably the most beloved of all U.S. presidents, Abraham Lincoln. The opening screen has links to six areas. Of those six, the Fact of the day, Quiz, and Museum in pictures areas provide the meat for this app. The Fact of the day offers both well-known and not so well-known facts about the president. During the month of February or while studying a unit on Abraham Lincoln, a teacher can ask the class to pull up this section.

The Quiz area has ten randomly selected questions, based on information in the Fact of the Day library. The directions explain that twenty seconds are allowed to answer each question. Throughout the quiz, there is a sound of a ticking clock, which is an actual recording of Lincoln's law office clock. A correct answer results in the sound of the Lincoln dinner bell, and an incorrect answer results in the sound of three gongs from Lincoln's clock. All sounds are authentic to the Abraham Lincoln Presidential Museum, in Springfield, Illinois, which developed this app.

The Museum in pictures page provides a good-quality pictorial tour of the museum. The remaining three areas are not for instructional purposes. The Contact link provides information about the Presidential Museum, such as entrance fees, address, phone numbers, and directions. The Gift Shop link offers a display of the books, T-shirts, and other items that are sold at the museum's gift shop. Finally, "High $5 Abe!" serves purely as a fund-raiser for the museum.

——ᴡᴡ——

Tiny Countries (recommended grades: 2–5)
TapToLearn Software
Website: www.taptolearn.com/
Cost: $0.99

The designers of this app created a scenario in which a rooster, named Dr. Evil, is attempting to move the continents of the world into positions that form the shape of a rooster. The mission of Tiny, the chicken, is to prevent that from happening. By playing this game, students can help Tiny thwart the efforts of Dr. Evil. A great deal of learning can take place with this app, about the locations of countries, their flags, major cities, and well-known monuments. Running the game in sections allows students to learn the material more fully.

The opening screen has an arrow to start the game. However, there are also Settings and Learn links, at the top, that should be checked first. The Settings allows users to turn off the sound and to designate the profile of the player. Teachers might want to show students the Learn area to familiarize them with the information about specific countries. The home screen for the Learn area shows the six major continents of the world. When students tap on a continent, the next window provides a list of all the countries on the continent.

If, for example, a student taps on Egypt, a screen comes up, as shown in Figure 5.4, which shows the location of the country, its capital and flag, other major cities, and any famous monuments. There is no need for students to learn all the facts initially, as portions of the Learn area are provided as needed throughout the game.

When students start the game, they see a cute introductory video that explains the missions of Dr. Evil and Tiny. There is a Skip button at the top if students have previously viewed the video. The mission is always to rescue the continent that is shown in red. After pressing Next, a Mission screen appears.

For the first portion of the game, Tiny is chasing Webster, who is working for Dr. Evil. An important Learn folder is provided on the right. Teachers can take a moment, at this point, to let students learn about the countries in a specific mission. For this part of the game, students need to know facts about the countries in a continent. If North America is the continent, the game requires information about Cuba, the United States, Canada, and Mexico.

After learning some facts, students press the GO button. After briefly seeing Webster hop on some countries, Tiny soon follows. However, Tiny cannot proceed until the correct country has been chosen in response to the question at the top of the screen, such as "Ottawa is the capital of which country?" Two options are provided.

If students select Canada, then Tiny proceeds on. However, if an incorrect answer is chosen, such as Cuba, Tiny then falls in the water, and the question remains. If Tiny falls in the water three times, a shark eats him, and the mission then needs to be restarted. That restart allows students to tap on the correct answer. After more than a dozen questions, the next screen provides a challenge to answer some additional questions.

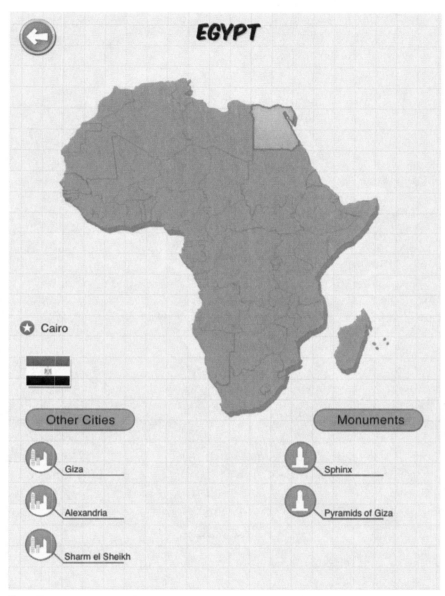

Figure 5.4. Learn area, Egypt

Periodically, there are short videos to keep students' attention. There are Time Out sessions, which give students time to study about countries that are covered in the next set of questions. Considerable learning can take place with this game.

Social Studies Apps for Middle School Students (Grades 5–8)

World Book—This Day in History for iPad (recommended grades: 6–12)
Software MacKiev
Website: www.mackiev.com/support.html
Cost: Free

This app provides a great bell-ringer activity. Students love to read the provided information. Learning the birthday of historic figures makes them more real. The information shared in This Day in History is not restricted to only history but also includes famous mathematicians and scientists, as well as key figures in all areas. Students who have a passion for singing will love knowing the birthday of Jenny Lynd, or student refugees from Uganda will be thrilled that the class is learning that their homeland became independent in 1962.

Figure 5.5 shows a typical page. January 30 has the birthday of a U.S. president and three important events from around the world. Tapping on the underlined names or events opens up a window with more detailed information. Sometimes, the window opens with associated music or speeches. For January 30, tapping on Roosevelt's name not only brings up the information about the president but also starts an audio excerpt from Roosevelt's first inaugural address. On other days, such as February 29, clips from *The Barber of Seville* are played after users tap on Rossini's name. The information provided with this app offers an excellent bell-ringer activity.

⟶⟶⟶

Lewis & Clark (recommended grades: 5–8)
Gibbs Smith Education
Website: www.gibbssmitheducation.com/lewisclark/
Cost: $1.99

The story of the Lewis and Clark expedition, commissioned by President Thomas Jefferson to try to find a Northwest Passage to the Pacific Ocean, has fascinated young learners for two centuries. This app provides ample information for unit studies, as well as semester projects.

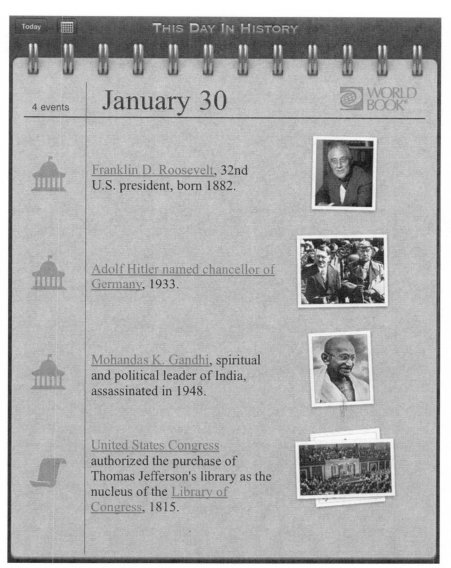

Figure 5.5. World Book—This Day in History

The opening screen includes links to the following seven areas:

- Overview
- Timeline
- Map
- Biographies

- Louisiana Purchase
- Supplies
- Discoveries

The Overview section provides seven pages with textual information; a graphic; and usually a sidebar with some fun facts, quotes, or discussion points. The second page of the Overview, shown in Figure 5.6, lists President Jefferson's goals for the expedition, as well as the names of the men whom he chose to serve on the expedition's corps. Those men would travel together for two years.

On the left menu is a story about Meriwether Lewis's dog, Seaman, and the explorer's devotion to his pet. Below are a couple of discussion questions from some of the other pages in the Overview area:

- Thomas Jefferson said, "Those who come afterwards will fill up the canvas we begin." What do you think he meant?
- After a year and a half the corps finally saw the Pacific. How do you think they felt?

The Timeline area follows events from the birth of Clark, on August 1, 1770, until his death on September 1, 1838. Other than the births and deaths of Lewis and Clark, the events all relate to the expedition itself. The easiest way to proceed through this area is to hold one finger down on the time line itself and slowly move to the right, which allows users to view each of the eighteen time periods along the way.

The Map area is interactive, showing the starting point, at St. Louis, to Fort Clatson on the Pacific Ocean, and also ten other stops along the way. As students tap on a specific location, information about the location pops up. If, for example, Fort Mandan is tapped, three dates are brought up with the events that are associated with that date at that fort.

The remaining four areas all share valuable information about this famous expedition. Another way to maneuver through this app is to tap at the bottom of any page; a scroll bar comes up, which allows for scrolling through the entire app.

━⟨∂∫∂⟩━

TapQuiz Maps World Edition (recommended grades: 5–12)
Rolzor
Website: www.rolzor.com/
Cost: Free or $0.99

The designers write that this app offers "an easy and quick way to learn World Geography." This is another app in which a great deal of learning can take place through the playing of a game. The home screen shows the major

This painting shows some members of Lewis and Clark's expedition.

Big Goals

Jefferson was excited and curious about the new western land. He sent a team of explorers to learn everything they could. He gave them these main goals:

* Make maps, especially of the rivers.
* Look for an all-water route to the Pacific Ocean. People hoped it existed, because it would make trading so much easier. (In those days travel by water was much easier than travel by land.) They called it the Northwest Passage.
* Make friends with the native peoples and learn about them. Let them know they are now part of the United States.
* Study the plants and animals.

A "Corps of Discovery"

Jefferson chose Meriwether Lewis to lead the team of explorers. Lewis was Jefferson's secretary and friend. He had been helping Jefferson plan for this special task already. Lewis needed a right-hand man to help him command the journey. He asked a friend from his army days, William Clark. Clark said yes.

Lewis and Clark gathered a group of 30–40 other men to join them. York, Clark's black slave, was part of the group. So was George Drouillard (drew-YAR), who was French and Shawnee. He could translate the French and Indain languages. He was also an excellent hunter and trapper.

Jefferson called the group the Corps of Discovery. A corps (kor) is a team of people working together.

Lewis took his dog, Seaman, on the journey. Once a Nez Perce chief asked to trade for Seaman. But Lewis could not part with his loyal friend. Lewis named a creek along their route for his dog so Seaman would always be remembered.

Gabe Stein, Publisher, Adobe, Illustration by Gary Kelleman

△ ○ ○○○○○○ ○ △

Figure 5.6.   Second page of information section

continents of the world, with the countries delineated by color. As an area of the world is tapped, a little blue window comes up that allows players to focus on a more specific region. For North America there are four regions, but Canada provides only one section of the provinces. The number of regions varies according to the specific area.

When students select a region, the area map comes up. A countdown alerts students that the game is about to commence. As the name of a country appears at the top, students should tap on the location of that country. If a correct answer is made, the word "Correct" temporarily appears, and students can move on. Similarly, an incorrect answer brings up the word "Incorrect," and students can guess again. If too much time is taken with an answer, a hint is provided by the appearance of a circle over the correct country.

Figure 5.7 shows the screen after all the South American countries have been identified accurately. Both the time and accuracy are shown at the top of the screen. The small brown window that comes up shows the accuracy percentage. The stars represent the time. Students are also given the option to Play Again. This game never gets boring as students strive for 100 percent accuracy, as well as the fastest possible time.

Altogether, there are twenty-two areas of the world that can be tested. Additionally, there is a Statistics link on the home page, which brings up an area that keeps a record of Overall Accuracy, Fastest time, and number of stars for each area test. From that Statistics page, there are also links that show the accuracy for each individual country, state, or province. Obviously, then, this app works best when played on the iPad by the same student. The Statistics area can be reset if teachers need to share the iPad with multiple students.

For only $0.99, this app has two additional features. First, students can actually type in the names of the countries onto the map. In addition, there is a Discovery Mode to find out the names. This feature would be good for studying prior to playing the game. And, of course, there are no advertisements on the paid version. With the free app, advertisements appear only on the home screen and not on the game screens, so they are certainly not that obtrusive.

—⁓—

The Revolution: Interactive Guide (recommended grades: 5–9)
Jeffrey Grimes
Website: www.linkedin.com/in/jeffgrimes9
Cost: Free

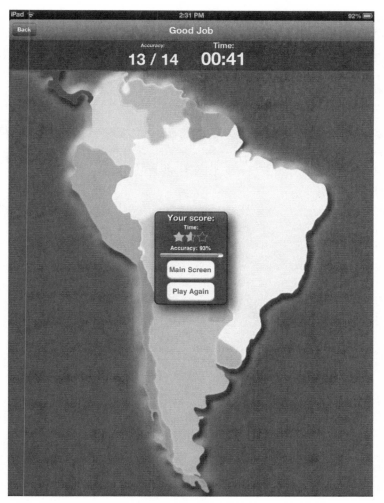

Figure 5.7. Completed quiz

This is an interactive textbook, designed by Jeffrey Grimes, as a senior project in high school. All but nine of the thirty-four pages have one or more interactive features. The first page, for example, has a recording accessed by tapping on the microphone icon, just to the right of the title, Pre-Revolution Patterns of Change. Each of the recordings in this app provides the learning objective for the section.

Also on the first page is an interactive box that explains five countries that were also enduring revolutions during the late eighteenth and early nineteenth centuries. The interactive features include flash cards, interactive maps, audio recordings, interactive boxes with related information, review quizzes, interactive biographies, and famous paintings with additional features.

Figure 5.8 shows a typical page with its interactive map. As time periods are selected, the map changes to show the areas of engagement or a related

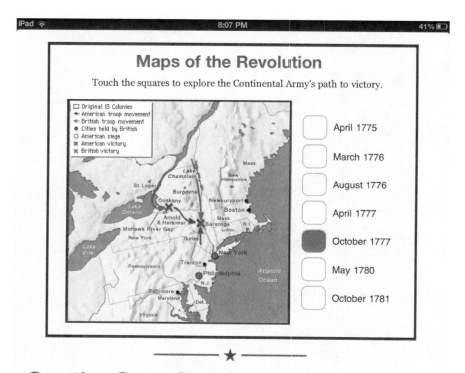

Creating State Governments

Of all the achievements of the Revolutionary era, among the most influential and long-lasting was the invention of the modern idea of a written constitution. This is a document that enumerates and limits the powers of government and safeguards the rights of the people.

Americans were the first modern people to regard a constitution as something separate from and superior to statute law. As such, a constitution could not be drafted by a legislature. It had to be produced by the people themselves. A constitution had to be drafted at a special convention, and then ratified by popular vote. The Massachusetts constitution, written by John Adams in 1780, is the oldest written constitution in continuous existence.

Figure 5.8. Sample page from app

picture. The following are the sixteen sections of this book, with the specific features:

- Pre-Revolution Patterns of Change (recording, map, two interactive boxes)
- The Effects of Colonial Tension (painting and quiz)
- The Boston Massacre & Boston Tea Party (interactive painting, another painting)
- The Seven Years' War (map)
- Modern Significance of the Revolution (interactive box, another box)
- American Society (interactive box, image of the Declaration of Independence)
- The Road to War (inactive flash cards)
- Explore: The Battles of Lexington and Concord (interactive painting)
- The Road to War; Declaring Independence (painting, interactive box)
- The War: Battles and Strategies (recording, two paintings, interactive box on Yorktown)
- The American Victory (map)
- Long-Term Impacts (recording, information box, interactive map)
- Creating State Governments
- The Founders (box to select information with pictures on eight founding fathers)
- The 1780s: Aftermath (interactive quiz).

This app is perfect for any middle school classroom that is delving into the American Revolution. The designer also created this video to give an overview of his app: youtube/YJbdrdEIcio

—⁓—

History 3D: Civil War (recommended grades: 7–12)
IggyCo, Inc.
Website: currently no designer website is available that has information about the app
Cost: $1.99

This app includes twenty-four images taken during the Civil War, from 1860 to 1865. The images were collected from the Library of Congress and can be viewed as black-and-white images, or, if 3-D glasses are available, the 3-D effects can be seen. The designers provided a title and a history with each image, as shown in Figure 5.9. At the bottom left of each picture is the toggle switch that changes the image's format from black-and-white to 3-D.

The information about the image pops up when students tap on the History button, at the bottom right. Tapping the little "i" button, at the

Figure 5.9. Image taken during the Civil War

top right, brings up information about the app's designers. Users can scroll through all the pictures by swiping right to left, just as one would turning the pages of a book. The home screen explains the information and shows a thumbnail of each picture, which serves as a direct link to an image. This is an excellent site for students to understand more about the conditions of the Civil War. For class reports, students can take a snapshot of the image, send it to themselves, and include it in their papers.

Social Studies Apps for
High School Students (Grades 9–12)

Timeline—U.S. History (recommended grades: 5–12)
Netsco
Website: netsco.kr/ (this is the company website, but it currently does not
    include any information about the app.)
Cost: Free

Time lines have tremendous value in providing students with a perspective of an entire time period and how events in that period relate to each other. This app covers 233 years of U.S. history, with events from July 4,

1776, when the United States declared its independence from Great Britain, to January 20, 2009, when Barak Obama was sworn in as president.

Figure 5.10 shows one small section of the time line. Tapping on any of the small thumbnail images along the time line brings up a detailed description of the event, as shown here for "The Star-Spangled Banner."

September 20, 1814

The U.S. national anthem "The Star-Spangled Banner" is first published in newspapers

"The Star-Spangled Banner" is the national anthem of the United States of America. The lyrics come from "Defense of Fort McHenry", a poem written in 1814 by the 35-year-old lawyer and amateur poet, Francis Scott Key, after witnessing the bombardment of Fort McHenry by the British Royal Navy ships in Chesapeake Bay during the Battle of Fort McHenry in the **War of 1812**.

The defense of Fort McHenry, which inspired "The Star-Spangled Banner"

The poem was set to the tune of a popular British song written by John Stafford Smith for the Anacreontic Society, a men's social club in London. "The Anacreontic Song" (or "To Anacreon in Heaven"), with various lyrics, was already popular in the United States. Set to Key's poem and renamed "The Star-Spangled Banner", it would soon become a well-known American patriotic song. With a range of one and a half octaves, it is known for being difficult to ____ gh the poem has four stanzas, only the first

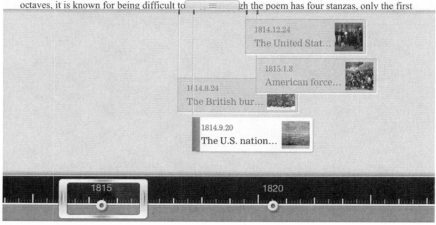

Figure 5.10.   Timeline with description of events

Users can quickly zoom along the time line to any date by tapping and dragging the rectangle at the bottom, which is hovering just past 1815 in the image above. Students can also scroll through the events more slowly by tapping on either side of the description area at the top of the app.

There are no activities associated with this app, but it provides an excellent opportunity to teach students how events are always impacted by what has come before.

⟶✦⟵

National Archives DocsTeach (recommended grades: 9–12)
National Archives and Records Administration
Website: docsteach.org/
Cost: Free; also available on Android

What a gem! This app focuses on creating activities that use original documents from the National Archives. Created first as a website, in 2010, the app equivalent was released in 2012. The opening page challenges users to "make sense of the past using documents from the National Archives." Two links are provided from the home page: Browse by Topic and Enter a Classroom Code. Tapping on the first link brings up a page with nine topics.

In addition to the ones shown in Figure 5.11, there are also the two topics Postwar U.S. 1945–early 1970s and Contemporary U.S. 1968–present. Tapping on any one of those nine topics brings users to a window that lists anywhere from two to six related activities. Altogether the app includes thirty-six premade activities. The Revolution & New Nation 1754–180 topic lists five subtopics. One activity topic, titled "To Sign or Not to Sign," allows students to step back in time and study the issues that confronted the members of the Continental Congress, concerning whether to sign the Declaration of Independence.

The activity provides an image of the Declaration of Independence, as well as details about the document. Students can zoom in to clearly see the writing as it appeared on the document. Teachers can challenge students with the four questions below, which are listed on the screen with the image of the Declaration of Independence:

1. Imagine that you are a member of the committee tasked with writing the Declaration of Independence. What is going through your mind as you draft the document?
2. How many of the thirteen colonies are represented at the bottom of the Declaration of Independence?

Now Viewing Topics

Civics & Government

Revolution & New Nation 1754-1820s

Expansion & Reform 1801-1861

Civil War & Reconstruction1850-1877

Rise of Industrial U.S. 1870-1890

Emergence of Modern U.S. 1890-1930

Great Depression & WWII 1929-1945

Figure 5.11. Listing of general topics

3. What do you think might explain why not all thirteen colonies are represented? Closely examine the last line of the document as you consider your answer.
4. If you were a member of the Second Continental Congress, would you have signed the Declaration of Independence? Why or why not? Remember to consider the risks and benefits!

While the above activity would work well for large-group discussions, some activities are best for individual use. The activity titled "Pearl Harbor

Time Line" instructs students to look and listen to nine original documents and then place them in chronological order. The document includes the original This is Not a Drill dispatch issued that morning of December 6, 1941. Also included are Roosevelt's original notes for his Day in Infamy speech to Congress.

The first website listed below is the original online DocsTeach home page. Teachers can register there and begin to create their own activities that use the available historic documents. A class code is created so the activity can then be used on the iPad.

Related Websites
- DocsTeach website: docsteach.org
- DocsTeach page for creating your own activity: docsteach.org/tools
- Blog with sample class code: blogs.archives.gov/online-public-access/?p=7829

⎯⎯⎯ഗ⎯⎯⎯

Google Earth (recommended grades: 5–12)
Google, Inc.
Website: support.google.com/earth/bin/answer.py?hl=en&answer=112749
Cost: Free; also available on Android

Google Earth was considered breathtaking when it was first released. Now, the novelty is gone a bit, but the value remains. The features provide a terrific tool for any high school history or geography class. This app addresses an acute need. Across the land, students who receive free and reduced lunches rarely have opportunities to travel outside their immediate area. This applies to students who live in large cities, as well as to students in rural areas.

For example, on a field trip from Nashville, Tennessee, to the National Air and Space Museum in Huntsville, Alabama, a student asked his teacher, "What direction will we have to go to get to Alabama?" Most students know the names of sports teams, but many have no idea of which states border their own home state. That information is probably studied in the lower grades, but it did not seem important to the students then. The maps in this app can captivate student attention. Students need an engaging way to learn about their states and countries and the world.

The opening screen shows the globe, as it slowly stretches across the full width of the screen. In the center of the top menu bar are three critical tools. Tapping on the N turns the globe so that it is oriented toward the north. Tapping on the icon just to the right of the N turns the globe, and then the image slowly zooms in to the location where the iPad and user currently are located. This feature brings the app down to "their world," and that is what engages students. The students can recognize their school. At the top right is a search area. Simply type in Sydney, Australia, for example, and the globe rotates and zooms into that city.

In the upper-left corner is a link to the drop-down Layers menu. Layers allows users to show specific features on a map. Users can choose as many of the features as are needed, although too many features will clutter the map. Eight features are provided:

- Places—A yellow box is provided for each place; when tapped more information appears.
- Businesses—A cross icon indicates a church, children for a school, a flag for a business.
- Panoramio Photos—A blue square indicates the location of an awesome picture of the location.
- Wikipedia—This brings up descriptions as they appear on Wikipedia.
- Borders and Labels—Provides typical map features.
- Roads—This feature shows interstates, as well as many small alleys.
- 3D Buildings—Thumbnail images can be tapped to show close-ups with details.
- Ocean—This doesn't label oceans but rather brings up locations, for example, the Coast Guard Marine Safety Lab.

Teachers should choose carefully the features that will be most valuable in any given lesson. The Search area is in the upper right. It recognizes street addresses, zip codes, and even names of many buildings. Figure 5.12 shows part of the image that was brought up when "Lipscomb University" was typed in the search area. The app found it, even without the state or city being provided.

The image here also shows a collection of images at the bottom. Those images can be accessed by tapping on a barely visible tab, which is directly in the middle, at the bottom of the screen. That brings up ten images that were taken in an area of perhaps a half-day's drive of where the map is showing. The images are actually videos that often show other related images.

The four websites below can give teachers ideas for using Google Earth in the classroom.

- YouTube Tutorial, 2/26/13: www.youtube.com/watch?v=id4v2sl92U4
- Good Earth user guide for the iPad: support.google.com/earth/bin/answer.py?hl=en&answer=112749

Figure 5.12.   Lipscomb University, with area pictures

- Google Earth Gallery: ratkacher.blogspot.com/2012/04/google-earth-ipad-app-more-than-meets.html
- iPad app guide for teachers: tips2012.edublogs.org/2012/06/27/tips-2012-ipad-app-guide-60-google-earth/

—⁓—

Flow of History Lite (recommended grades: 7–12)
John Butler
Website: www.flowofhistory.com/
Cost: $0.99 or $1.99

Many high school students seem to have a complete lack of knowledge about the sequence of time periods. This app allows students to understand the sequence of history and to realize how earlier events affect later time periods. The website states that this "app contains 243 interlinked flowcharts including a master flowchart and 17 unit flowcharts."

Figure 5.13 shows those seventeen units, both in the Master Flowchart, in the top of the screen, and the eighteen thumbnail images below, representing the introduction and the seventeen units. Every box on the Master Flowchart has a red circle with a black arrowhead; tapping on any box that has a circle like that takes users to another flowchart of the specified period. For example, tapping on Unit 14, Industrial Revolution, brings up a new flowchart that has eighteen categories, and each one has a red circle. Tapping on 14.6, Rising status of women, brings up another flowchart, with fourteen new topics, most of which lead to still more flowcharts.

The links continue, creating an interrelation between various topics. The numbers, such as 14.6, allow users to track their "locations" within a unit. The flowcharts in this app are always in the top part of the screen, and the unit images are in the bottom third of the screen. Those images allow users to go to the first flowchart specific to that time period. In other words, tapping on either of those images or on the corresponding unit in the Master Flowchart brings students to the exact same chart. However, the images can remain accessible, no matter what level; that is a good way to get back to the unit level.

The menu bar for this app is actually in the middle of the screen. Users can tap on the Reading button to access written information about the time period. Users can tap on the Flowchart button at any time to return to the default setting of the flowchart. On the right side of the menu bar, the Units button is the default setting.

However, when the user taps on the Timeline button, another set of small images replaces the unit images in the lower third of the screen. Those small images represent a significant event from the time period. Some areas will

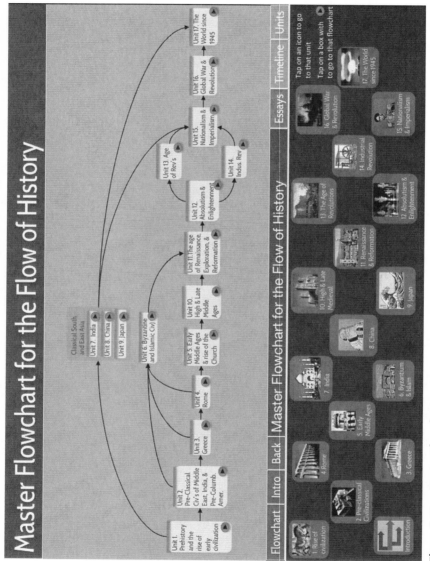

Figure 5.13. Master Flowchart

also have essays associated with them. There is a tremendous amount of history tucked into this one app. It is a terrific way to share with students the tremendously important "big picture" of any time period and how it relates to preceding and following time periods.

Website: YouTube introductory videos: www.youtube.com/watch?v=hl AfpQKSm-g

Note: Flow of History designers also developed the app Flow of History—World War I

——ᴏᴠᴏ——

Manual for the United States of America (recommended grades: 9–12)
Clint Bagwell Consulting
Website: cbagwellconsulting.com/usa2page.html
Cost: $1.99 for first edition or $5.99 for second edition

There are no gaming features here; this app is purely for obtaining facts and researching historic documents. The collection of information is a valuable resource for any high school history or government class. The home screen provides eight areas of study:

- Declaration of Independence
- The Constitution
- List of Presidents
- List of States
- Supreme Court Justices
- Supreme Court Cases
- U.S. Flag
- More Documents

The chart below gives a summary of the six areas available within the Declaration of Independence area alone:

- Main Text—This provides the exact text of the Declaration of Independence.
- Notes—This shows the time line of this document, from June 7 through August 2.
- Signers—Information is provided for each of the fifty-six signers of the Declaration.
- Original Parchment—This is an image of the original document. Zoom in to read.

- Engraving—This clearly shows the original writing. Use the two-finger spread to read.
- Declaration of Independence—John Trumbull's famous painting, made in 1818.

Then the Constitution area offers links to thirty-five areas, which include:

- The Preamble
- The seven articles of the Constitution
- The original ten amendments (Bill of Rights)
- The remaining twenty-seven amendments
- Proposed amendments, not yet ratified by the states
- A list of the original signers
- Biographies of the original signers, in a format similar to the area for signers of the Declaration, shown in Figure 5.14
- Images of five original documents, including the Bill of Rights

Also, the final link shows the famous painting "Scene at the Signing of the Constitution of the United States," by Howard Chandler Christy, and includes a link to nine paragraphs that give details about the painting. Similar details are available in all the remaining links from the home page. Certainly, do not miss the More Documents area. The eighteen documents there include:

- Articles of Confederation
- Federalist Papers

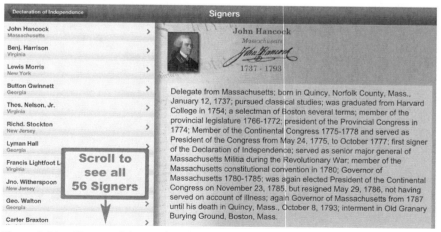

Figure 5.14. Signers of the Declaration of Independence

- Anti-Federalist Papers
- Washington's Farewell Address
- Louisiana Purchase Treaty
- Treaty of Guadalupe Hidalgo
- Emancipation Proclamation
- Gettysburg Address
- Lincoln's Second Inaugural Address
- United Nations Charter
- How Our Laws Are Made
- Censure of Senator McCarthy
- Nuclear Test Ban Treaty
- Civil Rights Act
- Indian Bill of Rights
- Patriot Act
- American Recovery Reinvestment Act

What a resource this offers, all in one location! As students peruse this app, they can begin to understand how our county developed and pulled together as a nation. If money is available, the second edition of this app magnifies the amount of information available, but the first edition alone is definitely worthy of being selected as one of the top five apps for the social studies classroom.

Apps Appropriate for the History Classroom, but Described Elsewhere

Middle School: Free Books
Cost: Free, $0.99, or $3.99

Discussed in chapter 4 of this book, this app provides 23,469 classics to go. Because several subjects are listed in the library area, this app could also be used in social studies classes. Three related topics that are listed are history, politics, and war.

—⟋∞⟍—

High School: Constitution and Federalist Papers
Multieducator Inc.
Free

Discussed in chapter 4 of this book, this app not only provides every word from the U.S. Constitution, but related documents are also included, such as the Federalist Papers, all twenty-seven amendments, and more.

⎯⎯⎯⎯⎯⎯

High School: PrepZilla Study with Friends Game
gWhiz, LLC
Cost: Free

Discussed in chapter 2 of the second book in this set, this app's topics include AP European history, AP human geography, AP U.S. government and politics, AP U.S. history, AP world history, and regents exam: global history.

⎯⎯⎯⎯⎯⎯

Middle School: Geo Walk HD—3D World Fact Book
Vito Technology, Inc.
Cost: $0.99

Discussed in the middle school area of chapter 3 of the second book in this set, Geo Walk provides more than 580 pictures in three main categories: Places, Flora and Fauna, and People. The Places and People categories are perfect for social studies classes at both the middle school and high school levels.

Additional Highly Rated History Apps

Since such a broad range of subjects resides under the umbrella of social studies, choosing the top five listed above was indeed a challenge. Below are fifteen others in this also-ran section. All are appropriate for high school or middle school, except Ansel & Clair: Paul Revere's Ride, which is more appropriate for the elementary or middle school level.

U.S. Presidents and the Presidency
Presidents Quizzer
Supergonk, Ltd.
Cost: Free

This is a great app! The only reason for not including it above is that it is primarily a collection of games on the presidency and the United States in general. Some additional quizzes are available for $0.99.

⎯⎯⎯⎯⎯⎯

Thud! Presidents
Ball & Sprocket, LLC
Cost: Free or $2.99

This is another fun game!

US President (American Presidents Life History)
Nirmala TV
Cost: $0.99

There are quite a few apps with information about our presidents, but this is one of the best.

American History
Civil War: 1863 Lite
Hunted Cow Studios, Ltd.
Free or $1.99

This is an excellent game, appropriate for middle or high school.

Civil War Today
A&E Television Mobile Network
Cost: $0.99

Excellent!

Ansel & Clair: Paul Revere's Ride
Cognitive Kid, Inc.
Cost: $4.99

This app is wonderful for upper-elementary and middle school. The price is the only reason this is not included in the apps above.

Battle of Gettysburg
Multieducator Inc.
Cost: $0.99

This app includes sixty high-quality photos and drawings, ten maps, ten firsthand accounts, and a six-minute video.

Other Cultures
European Exploration
GAMeS Lab at RU
Cost: Free

This is a fun game in which students are asked to build and outfit ships prior to a cross-seas expedition.

⚬⚬⚬

Virtual History Roma
Arbikdi Mondadory Editore, S.p.A.
Cost: $8.99
This highly rated app "provides the viewer with an astonishing insight into Roman civilization, using innovative functions and multimedia content: from the spectacular digital reconstruction of the city's statues to breathtaking aerial views of the metropolis as it stood 2,000 years ago."

⚬⚬⚬

The Pyramids
Touch Press
Cost: $6.99
Students have always been fascinated with the pyramids. The price is the only reason this highly rated app is not reviewed within this chapter.

Miscellaneous
Britannica Kids
Encyclopedia Britannica, Inc.
Cost: $4.99
This is actually a collection of apps, each costing $4.99 and each covering a specific time period, for example, the Aztec empire, rainforests, U.S. presidents, ancient Egypt, endangered species, volcanoes, and dinosaurs.

⚬⚬⚬

History: Maps of the World
Seungbin Cho
Cost: Free
This is rated only three stars. However, the app provides, at no cost, 180 maps from a wide range of time periods and cultures.

⚬⚬⚬

Sphere—360 Camera
Spark Labs
Cost: Free

This is a MUST try! There are innumerable panoramic scenes from around the world AND you can shoot your own. More ideas for using this in the classroom: appedreview.org/sphere-360-camera/

———

Classical World Lite: History Challenge
Maple Leaf Soft
Cost: Free or $0.99

The free version provides twenty questions about the Greek and Roman Empires; the paid version has 202 questions. This is highly rated, but it is purely a quiz. Other history challenge apps are also available for the American Revolution, the Civil War, World War I, World War II, U.S. presidents, Hitler's Germany, Cold War life, the American military, and Napoleon.

———

History
A&E Television Networks Mobile
Cost: Free

This is an awesome collection of videos that have been viewed on the History Channel. These are also available on the web.

Reflections on Chapter 5

So the word "memorize" has not been mentioned with a single one of these apps. They were each designed to captivate students' attention with vivid imagery of times past. The apps in the elementary areas are mostly about games so that students can enjoy the fun and challenge of learning through gaming.

The apps in the middle school area represent four vastly different ways for bringing history to life. As shown below, those techniques include a bell-ringer activity, gaming, interactive textbooks, and a photo album.

- Bell-ringer activity: World Book—This Day in History
- Gaming—TapQuiz maps
- Two interactive textbooks—The Revolution: Interactive Guide and Lewis & Clark
- Photo album—History 3D: Civil War

The apps in the high school area recognize the need for incorporating more research from original documents, with both National Archives

DocsTeach and Manual for the United States of America. Students can also begin to understand the sequence of historic events by using both the Timeline—U.S. History app, which focuses on U.S. history, and the Flow of History app, which covers world events from the beginning of time. As students learn about events from any of those apps, they can check the location of the event on Google Earth.

The apps in this chapter let students begin to love history. By loving history, they will grow to appreciate those who have gone before and the sacrifices that so many have made to bring our world to the state in which we find ourselves today.

For those who are interested in keeping up with significant changes that relate to these apps, as well as learning about new history-related apps, I have created a private wiki. Directions for being a member of the wiki are provided in the introduction to this book.

CHAPTER SIX

———~⁄⁄⁄~———

Teaching Foreign Languages
with the iPad

Introduction

This chapter presented a unique challenge. What languages should be included? Certainly Spanish deserves considerable attention because it is taught in most U.S. schools that have a foreign language curriculum. However, recent trends indicate that some school districts are dropping French and German and bringing in Mandarin Chinese. A study by the Center for Applied Linguistics, in 2008, shows the languages offered by schools with foreign language programs, both in 1997 and 2008.

In Figure 6.1, data is provided for only the secondary level, but trends at the elementary level were similar. The dark bars show the status for 2008. Obviously, the distribution chart shows clearly that Spanish far surpasses all other languages, with 93 percent of the schools that provide a foreign language offering Spanish. French still remains the second most frequently taught language, but the percentages were markedly decreasing from 1997 until 2008.

In fact, at both the elementary and secondary levels, the teaching of French, German, and Italian decreased, whereas the teaching of Chinese and some other languages has shown significant increases. Research shows that the gain in the number of schools that offer Mandarin Chinese reflects a national trend (Koebler, 2011). Considering both the current numbers and the recent trends, the decision was made to focus in this chapter on the top six languages at the secondary level.

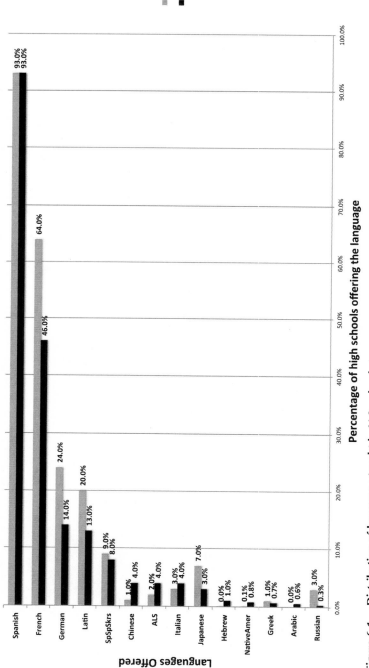

Figure 6.1. Distribution of languages taught in U.S. schools

Source: Used by permission of N. C. Rhodes and I. Pufahl (2009). Foreign language teaching in U.S. schools: Results of a national survey. Executive summary. Washington, DC: Center for Applied Linguistics.

For Spanish, four apps are covered, and the remaining five languages have two apps each. In addition, a chart is provided near the end of the chapter that lists highly rated, free apps for other languages. That chart includes twenty-one apps for six additional languages. Altogether this chapter includes apps for a dozen languages. For those interested in reading more about the current offerings and trends concerning foreign language instruction in U.S. schools, six websites are listed at the end of the chapter, each providing an interesting perspective.

Rather than organizing the chapter into elementary, middle, and high school sections, as has been done in the two previous chapters, this chapter is divided into languages, with recommendations for beginner, intermediate, or advanced. No apps are included for Spanish for Spanish Speakers (SpSpSpkrs). The curriculum in those courses focuses more on grammar rules, as well as on writing and reading Spanish. All except the first app in the Spanish section would be equally appropriate for Spanish speakers.

Readers should also check two other apps that have already been discussed in this book. Logic Advance is discussed in chapter 2 of *The Deuce and a Half iPad*. Although that chapter is about mathematics, the app allows users to set the language to Spanish, French, Russian, or Ukrainian. Also, as discussed in chapter 3 of this book, Audio Memos is a great way for students to make recordings of themselves while speaking a foreign language. Those recordings can be emailed to teachers or saved to compare with later recordings as students improve with pronunciations.

Spanish Language Apps

Learn Spanish (recommended level: beginning)
MindSnacks
Website: www.mindsnacks.com/help/
Cost: Free or $4.99

When first opening this app, users are asked to create an account with name, email, and password. The app explains that it needs the sign-in to function as a "full-featured learning coach." The sign-in occurs only once but can be changed later for other users. Accounts can be set up through Facebook or email. The home screen has a menu, accessed from the upper-left corner. That drop-down menu provides links to the following areas:

- Home
- Profile

- Quests
- Settings
- Switch User

To get started from the home screen, users tap on the cute fish, named Swell, to bring up the first learning activity. A single word, such as "two," appears at the top of the screen, with two choices provided below, such as "dos" and "doce." The YouTube video listed below shows the game, as it appears on an iPhone. At the end of the activity, the words on which students were tested are shown, with green bars indicating how close the students are to mastering the word. Students can tap on the Scorecard link at the very bottom to practice identifying the words and to listen to the correct pronunciations.

The fish Swell represents level 1. On the home screen, next to Swell, the cute frog, named Belly, represents level 2. Words become a bit more advanced. Figure 6.2 shows one page with a selection of figures. As students proceed through the levels, the number of items increases. Students hear a voice pronounce the word that appears at the top of the screen. Students should tap on the correct image. After a selection has been made, the frog at the bottom of the screen extends its tongue to digest it. The item is minimized in the frog's stomach. If the selection is incorrect, the frog cannot digest the image.

After several minutes of play, the ending screen shows students' high scores. Tapping on the screen opens an area that shows how well the words were mastered. Trouble Words are identified so students know which words to study. On the upper-right corner of the home page is a link to a study area. Blue bars by words indicate that the word has been mastered. Other bars indicate how far along students are to mastery. The picture of every word can be tapped to hear the correct pronunciation.

The link on the upper left of the home screen brings up a menu to the following areas.

- Lessons—with bars to indicate how well a word has been learned
- Profile—shows eight indicators of progress, for example, words mastered, lessons learned, active days
- Quests—ways to earn extra points in the games
- Settings—various available, as well as a link to the online help pages
- Switch User—Obviously, very useful for shared iPads

Figure 6.2. Level 2 selections

As the words are learned, other levels of the game are unlocked. Nine levels are available with this free app, and each level brings up an entirely different game. For more advanced users, fifty lessons can be purchased for $4.99.

Video on level 1: www.youtube.com/watch?v=UdvX62baOaM

Note: MindSnacks also has apps available in French, Italian, Mandarin Chinese, Portuguese, and German.

⸻◦◦◦⸻

ConjuVerb—Spanish Verb Conjugation Helper
Codepoet, LLC (recommended levels: beginning and intermediate)
Website: conjuverb.com/
Cost: Free

Anyone who has studied Spanish knows that learning the many forms of Spanish verbs can be *muy difícil*. This app provides a good way to review and begin to understand the conjugation of more than six hundred of the most commonly used Spanish verbs. Even native speakers can have trouble with conjugations, so this app is beneficial for both regular Spanish classes and classes for Spanish speakers.

The opening screen is deceptively banal, showing just a blank page, with a search bar at the top. To get started, users type a word in the search area and then tap on either the Spanish or English word. For example, if students want to learn about the Spanish verbs for "run," they should type "run" into the search area and then tap on the English button, below. The app then provides links to various forms of *correr*.

Tapping on any of those links fills the screen with conjugations for Presente, Pretérito, Futuro, Imperfecto, Condicional, Presente Perfecto, Futuro Perfecto, Pluscuamperfecto, Pretérito Anterior, and Condicional Perfecto. Other areas, available from the top menu, are Indicativo, Subjuntive, Imperativo, and Otras Formas. Similarly, students can tap on Spanish, on the home screen, and then type in a Spanish verb.

On the bottom menu, as shown in Figure 6.3, there are four options: Search, Flash Card, Words, and More. Tapping on the Flash Card section brings up a settings page, with many options for personalizing the cards. Students may choose Starred, Recent, All, or Top 75 words. Within those selections, tenses can be selected. To start, users press the Go button, at the bottom, which brings up the first word. At the top right, a toggle switch allows users to select whether they want the Spanish word or the English translation first. Tapping the screen flips the card, and swiping to the left goes to the next word.

The Words section is another valuable area. Again four selections are provided at the bottom: Recent, Starred, All, or Top. This is an excellent study area. Students can review by covering the words on the left or right side and then checking for accuracy. Tapping within any of the horizontal lines brings up the conjugation of the verb.

The More area is a settings area. The Theme area allows for a change in the background of the Flash Cards. In the Vosotros area, all the vosotros

Figure 6.3. ConjuVerb Flash Card

verbs throughout the app can be hidden. There are other options, including FAQ, which links to the FAQ area of the ConjuVerb website.

—⌀⌀⌀—

Free Spanish English Dictionary + (recommended levels: all)
Ascendo, Inc.
Website: www.ascendo-inc.com/spanish-english-dictionary-iphone-ipad.html
Cost: Free or $9.99; also available on Android

This app provides much more than a dictionary. Perhaps "a dictionary on steroids" would be an appropriate definition. The plus sign at the end to the ti-tle refers to the availability of text-to-speech pronunciation, phrasebook, verb conjugator, full-length text translator, and a vocabulary quiz generator. The opening screen has a pop-up window, inviting users to add even more features. Users can try the free version first and then add features as needed. The paid version eliminates the commercial bar that is near the bottom of each screen.

The bottom menu offers links to seven areas. The Dictionary area opens initially. At the top of the left column is the Search area. Below that is a list of all the words included with this app, both in English and Spanish. To the right of the search area are six buttons, the first of which is a microphone. After tapping there, a recording can be made of users speaking the Spanish word. The arrow next to the microphone allows for a playback of the recording. The next icon is a camera that takes pictures of anything users wish to use as a picture at the bottom of the selection of words that are being viewed.

For example, users can place a picture of a staircase on the page that defines *escalera*. Students can select a picture by tapping on the icon just to the right of the camera, which accesses the Photos area of the iPad. The other two icons on the top menu bar are for mailing the page and writing notes. Teachers can require that students write notes below a word and then email those notes to them.

The next area linked from the bottom menu is the Phrases area. On the right side of this area are expressions in both English and Spanish that relate to one of twenty areas that can be selected on the left. In Figure 6.4, Asking Directions has been selected, with five pairs of phrases showing on the right. Eight additional phrases are available below those initial five.

The next area linked from the bottom menu is the Verbs area, which provides the conjugation of all the verbs that are in the dictionary. Next on the

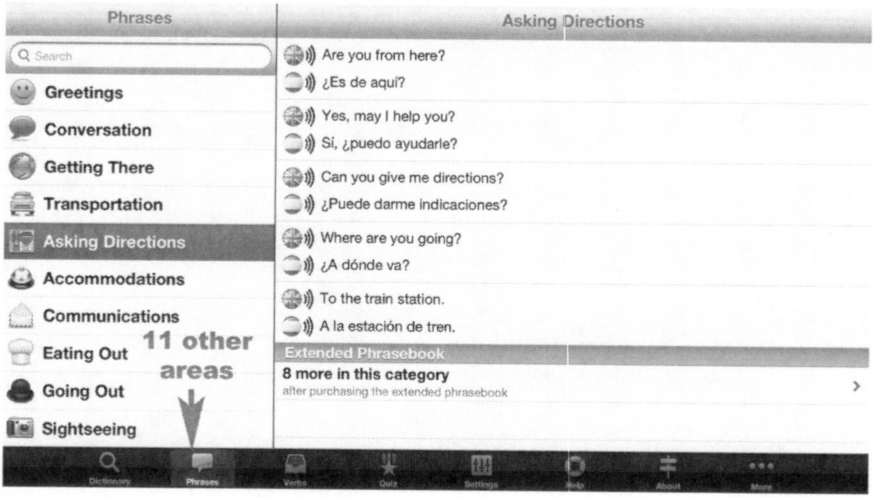

Figure 6.4. Phrases for asking directions

menu is the star; this leads to the Quiz area, which can be set to show Spanish or English words, with four possible answers. An accurate answer will bring up a Correct window. Similarly, a wrong answer brings up an Incorrect window, in which the correct answer is provided.

The remaining links on the bottom menu are Settings, Help, About, and More. The More area is where users can purchase additional features or, for $7.99, purchase the full version. The full version undoubtedly eliminates the constantly changing commercials.

Note: Ascendo, Inc., also publishes dictionaries in French, Italian, and German.

―――

teleSUR (recommended levels: intermediate and advanced)
teleSUR
Website: exwebserv.telesurtv.net/secciones/canal/contactenos.php
Cost: Free; also available on Android

Telesur is a Latin American news app, which provides a large collection of short videos. This app can be immensely helpful in moving Spanish learners beyond the basic levels of learning Spanish by increasing their understanding of the spoken word. Everything on this app is entirely written in Spanish, and the videos are also entirely in Spanish.

As shown in Figure 6.5, below a major news story of the day, the home screen also has a collection of twenty-four short video clips arranged in rows of six categories.

The categories are shown on the left side and include Politics, Economics, Sports, Culture, Science, and Environment. Within each category, fifteen videos can be accessed. Each video has a short description below it and usually runs for less than a minute, although some can occasionally be as long as ten to twelve minutes.

When users tap on a specific video, a new window pops up with a full paragraph description. They can acccess full-screen viewing of the video by tapping on the thumbnail in that new window. Below the description, categories are provided that relate to the video. Each brings up an extended list of videos that provide background to related areas. Also on the pop-up window are tabs to share (*compartir*) or download (*descargar*) the video. Additionally, below those two links, there may be one or more videos that specifically relate to the selected video.

At the very top of the home screen, as shown in Figure 6.5, there are seven icons. Tapping on the globe brings up a map of the world, with pins that indicate locations of a news stories. If users tap on a specific pin, a small

Figure 6.5. Home screen of teleSUR

pop-up window comes up, with a title of the story. Tapping on the blue arrow brings up a full window, exactly as explained in the previous paragraph.

The next three icons bring up videos from television (*programas*), documentaries (*documentales*), and reports (*reportajes*). The videos available in those areas are longer than the short videos available from the home screen.

There is also a search area available on the top menu. The last section, Más, provides information about teleSUR, as well as connections to Facebook, Twitter, and YouTube.

Spanish professors and teachers often encourage their students to watch a Spanish TV station to improve our ability to understand the spoken language. This app has an even greater advantage for students, as the videos can quickly be paused or replayed. Also, related videos can be watched, and written descriptions can assist in the understanding.

Another Highly Rated App for Teaching Spanish

Duolingo
Cost: Free

This is a highly rated app that provides activities in five languages: Spanish, German, French, Portuguese, and Italian.

French Language Apps

Learn French with busuu! (recommended levels: beginning and intermediate)
busuu, Limited
Website: www.busuu.com/enc/mobile
Cost: Free, $4.99, or $16.99; also available on Android

The opening screen has six selections on the left menu, although the first, Course Selection, is where the bulk of users' time will be spent. That section provides the options of Beginner A1, Beginner A2, Intermediate B1, or Intermediate B2. Each of those provides two subareas, with three free lessons each. Below the free lessons are a dozen or more for-pay lessons, such as Numbers, Personal Pronouns, and Colors. Altogether twenty-four free lessons come with this app. To have access to all the premium lessons costs $16.99. An additional busuu.com French travel course is included with the $16.99 fee, or it can be purchased separately for $4.99.

Within Course Selections, if area A1.1 is selected, the free lessons are titled:

- Nice to meet you!
- How are you?
- To be or not to be

Tapping on "Nice to meet you!" brings up a screen, as shown in Figure 6.6, with the buttons that provide links to the four areas. The black arrows

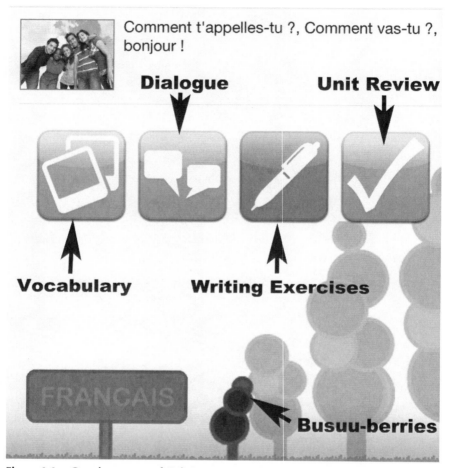

Comment t'appelles-tu ?, Comment vas-tu ?, bonjour !

Dialogue **Unit Review**

Vocabulary **Writing Exercises**

FRANÇAIS

Busuu-berries

Figure 6.6.   Opening screen of "Nice to meet you!" area

and labels were added for the convenience of readers. Those four areas are provided on every lesson. A green color indicates that the area has been completed. Otherwise the area is red.

In the Vocabulary area a new French word is shown, with an associated picture and its translation. There is also a button to press to hear the correct pronunciation. A few new words and a small quiz test users' ability to recognize one of the words. The Dialogue area plays a recording of a conversation. The text of the conversation is also shown. After pressing the Start button at the bottom, students are provided with three questions, after which the correct and incorrect answers will be shown. If all three were not correct, then students can try again, from the start.

In the Dialogue section, students first listen to a conversation between two or three people, and the text of the conversation is shown. Then, by tapping on the Start button, a short three-question quiz follows. The Writing Exercise requests users to be logged in to write a paragraph of a conversation in which they introduce a friend to another person. The Unit Review has ten questions. Some questions relate to identifying pictures, and others require users to drag and drop words over the correct translation or drag words to build a sentence.

The Continue Course button, on the home screen, allows students to return to a previously studied area. By entering the My Mistakes area, students can study words that were previously missed. Beginning with the My Correction area, the next three links are online features. The fifth item on the opening screen's left menu is titled Login/Register. This brings up options to obtain other busuu apps. The last menu item allows users to sign up to join busuu's language-learning community through Facebook or email.

Note: busuu currently publishes twenty-four language-related apps; most are free and others are $4.99.

—⁓—

French 24/7 Language Learning (recommended levels: beginning and intermediate)
24/7 Tutor, Inc.
Website: www.247tutor.com/
Cost: Free or $5.99 each for additional Vocabulary and additional Phrases

What a terrific idea to have a tutor 24/7! The opening screen of this app provides links to five main categories:

- Home & Family
- Town & Country
- Opposites
- Basic Phrases
- Questions

Figure 6.7 shows the home screen for the Home & Family category. The Categories button returns users to the home screen. The two red buttons at the top, on the next level below Categories, are for adding vocabulary and phrases, for additional fees. Tapping on any of the other four home screen links brings up similar screens. An excellent place to start is to tap on the tiny "i," at the bottom of the screen, which opens a screen titled "Tips on using 24/7 Tutor." Several good suggestions are included there. Then the

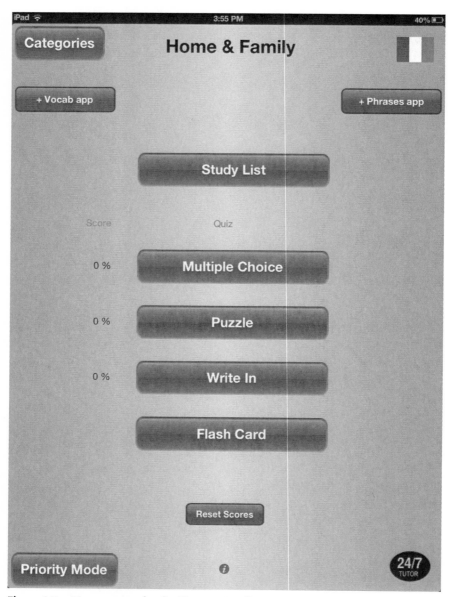

Figure 6.7. Home screen for the Home & Family category

Study List button brings up a list of twenty-five words. Users can tap on the word to hear the correct pronunciation.

The next four areas provide ways to practice the words that were provided in the Study List. In the Multiple Choice area students are shown a word, such as "*le lit*" and then have a choice of five possible answers. After tapping an answer, students then need to tap on the Answer button at the bottom. A correct answer brings a green, happy smiley face, and then a Next button replaces the Answer button. An incorrect answer shows a red, sad emoticon. When the quiz is done, students have the option to "record" the score or not.

From the home screen, the Puzzle area provides an excellent opportunity to become more familiar with the basic vocabulary. An English word appears at the top of the screen, and dashes appear below that, indicating the number of letters in the French translation. The Write In section requires an even greater knowledge of the words. The English word again appears at the top, but this time students are expected to type in the entire word. The only clues are the dots below the writing area, which indicate the number of letters needed. If users type in a correct letter, a circle replaces the dot. An incorrect letter shows an "x" in place of the dot.

Finally, the Flash Cards are a bit different from the normal flash cards that flip when tapped. Here, an English word appears at the top. Settings are provided below that allow users to have the sound played and words appear automatically. With both of those settings off, users have an icon, in the lower right, that plays the sounds, and an answer/next button is provided to show the answer and then proceed to the next word.

Additional Highly Rated Apps for Teaching French

Free French English Dictionary +
Ascendo, Inc.
Cost: Free or $9.99
Works just like the Spanish app by Ascendo, discussed earlier in this chapter.

——ᴔ∕∕ᴔ——

Learn French
MindSnacks
Cost: Free
This app works just like the Spanish app by MindSnacks, listed as the first app in this chapter.

——ᴔ∕∕ᴔ——

Learn French—Très Bien
Online Language Help
Cost: Free
This app is also highly rated.

—◦◦◦—

Duolingo
Cost: Free
This highly rated app provides learning activities in five languages: Spanish, German, French, Portuguese, and Italian.

German Language Apps

Learn German—Wie Geht's (recommended level: beginner)
Online Language Help
Website: www.wiegehtsgerman.com
Cost: Free or $9.99; also available on Android
The opening screen shows eight areas of study, although only the Beginner and Glossary sections are available with the free version. Twenty-seven sections are included in the Beginner area; Figure 6.8 shows links to nearly half of those. Unfortunately, only seventeen areas are free. After the two Color sections, other sections include:

- Family
- Extended Family
- Describing People
- Numbers (0–10)
- Numbers (11–19)
- Numbers (20–100)
- Numbers (100–1,000,000)
- Ordinal Numbers
- Days of the week
- Months & Seasons
- Holidays
- Human body
- Human body II
- Animals (Mammals)
- Animals (Others)

Within the How Are You? section, fourteen German expressions are provided, which all relate to initial greetings that one might say when meeting someone, either formally or informally. Exact translations and a button to hear the correct pronunciation are also provided. At the top are links to the Lesson area and the Hangman area.

For a typical lesson, a word appears at the top, a recording plays the correct pronunciation, and four possible answers are shown below. If students select the correct answer, that answer is circled in green and a Correct! message appears below the word. An incorrect answer is crossed out in red, and users must tap the circled correct answer to continue.

The Hangman area, mentioned above, provides a fun way to review newly learned words and phrases. Students can miss up to seven times before a

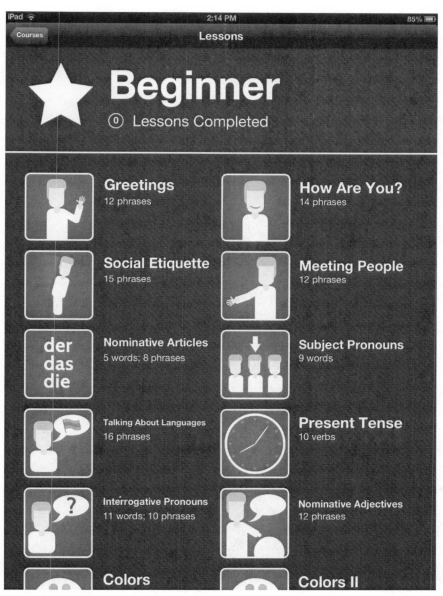

Figure 6.8. Beginner area

recording plays the correct pronunciation of the expression. If students are successful with this game "Sehr gut!" (You win!) appears on the screen, and again the recording plays the correct pronunciation.

——⁓⁓⁓——

Die Der Das Lite (recommended level: beginner)
Mobomind Kotnik, K.D.
Website: www.diederdas.net/
Cost: Free or $1.99

Learning a new language can be difficult. However, for German, learning the correct article that should be paired with all the nouns only exacerbates some of the struggles that new learners have to overcome. German has three genders: masculine (der), feminine (die), and neutral (das). This app provides an excellent way for reviewing articles that match German nouns. The free version of the app has thirty-six nouns, whereas the paid version has more than seven hundred.

Figure 6.9 shows a lesson in process. The user has correctly answered four questions and missed one. The user now must make the correct choice for the word "Staat." The word is the sixth word in the lesson, and the translation of the word is below the number six. A correct answer is indicated by a green check mark. An incorrect answer briefly shows the correct answer, before placing the pink "x" on the score sheet. If the sound is left on during the lesson, an incorrect answer also triggers a recording of the correct answer. The menu at the bottom allows students to restart the lesson, to proceed to a

Figure 6.9. Halfway through one lesson

new lesson, or to toggle the sound on or off. This app is straightforward and a great tool for new learners of the German language.

Additional Highly Rated Apps for Teaching German

Learn German—MindSnacks, Learn German with busuu!, and German FREE 24/7 Language Learning are all highly rated apps for learning German. These are not described in this section only because the same apps, for different languages, were discussed previously.

—◦◦◦—

Free German English Dictionary +
Ascendo, Inc.
Cost: Free and $9.99
 This app works just like the Spanish app by Ascendo, discussed earlier in this chapter.

—◦◦◦—

German
Nguyen Van Thanh
 This is a dictionary app, which is also highly rated.

—◦◦◦—

Duolingo
Cost: Free
 This highly rated app provides learning activities in five languages: Spanish, German, French, Portuguese, and Italian.

Latin Language Apps

Latin + (recommended levels: beginner to advanced)
Paul Hudson
Website: www.romansgohome.com/
Cost: $0.99
 This app is a teaser for the more inclusive and highly rated app SPQR Latin Dictionary and Reader. Unfortunately, SPQR is expensive ($6.99), especially for using with one-on-one initiatives. iTunes describes that app as "the ultimate learning tool for Latin students who want to immerse themselves in the language, presenting the most comprehensive Latin dictionary on the App Store, dozens of Latin texts with English translations, a grammar

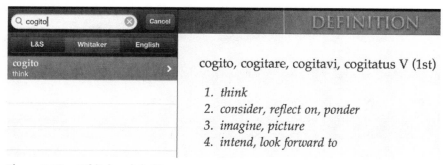

Figure 6.10. Whitaker definition

tester, flashcards, quiz, numeral converter, quotes of ancient wisdom, language learning tools and more."

This Latin app is purely the dictionary portion of its more expensive cousin. The opening screen presents a search area, at the top left of the screen. When a word is typed in the search area, the definition comes up, based on information from the well-known Lewis and Short Latin Dictionary. All the abbreviations that appear throughout the definition can be quite intimidating to new Latin scholars. They refer to ancient authors and the works where the specific word is used. If used in advanced classes, the website below is a good resource, as it explains the meaning of those abbreviations.

The Whitaker tab provides definitions simpler than those from the Whitaker Latin Dictionary, as shown in Figure 6.10. Those definitions are much more appropriate for first-year students. The final tab allows students to type in English words to come up with the Latin definition. If "learn" is typed in the search area, then the left area fills with thirty-two possibilities; all the possibilities relate to the word "learn," for example, learn, learn about, learn by heart, learn in advance. Tapping on any one of the terms on the left side brings up details about the word, such as tenses.

If funds are available, advanced Latin students should definitely consider the full version. The website above includes a video that explains the various additional features.

Abbreviations used in the Lewis and Short Latin Dictionary are explained here: latinlexicon.org/LNS_abbreviations.php

Latin (recommended levels: beginner and intermediate)
Paul Hudson
Website: www.romansgohome.com/apps
Cost: $0.99

At the App Store, Mr. Hudson currently holds the record for designing the most apps for classical languages. Specifically, thirty-two of his apps address Latin, Greek, and Bible studies. SPQR and Latin + are currently his highest-rated Latin apps. This Latin app is not as highly rated, but it provides some gaming features that can add some levity to the study of a language that many students consider dull.

The opening screen provides the option of playing the game at three levels: Easy, Medium, or Hard. Also, there is a brief How to Play paragraph, as follows: "You will be given the English meanings of seven Latin words; you need to make those words by tapping matching letter tiles."

New learners appreciate that there are no time limits and no penalties for incorrect answers. The mission of the game is to allow students to become familiar with Latin words and phrases. After selecting Easy and then pressing Go, students are brought to the next screen, which has fifty boxes. Each box represents a quiz. After students successfully complete a quiz, a star is placed on the corresponding box.

Each set of words can be played more than once, but no additional stars are added. After tapping on a numbered box, the game begins. Each game screen shows seven English words, with the number of letters in the Latin translation provided on the side to assist students. Then, at the bottom of the screen are combinations of two or three letters that students use to spell the word correctly. As the correct combination of letters is selected, letters are removed from the lower level. As students tap on the green Go tab, if the spelling is correct, the word takes its position across from the English translation.

For example, Figure 6.11 shows one game in which the user has finished the four Latin words, which are in place next to the English translation. Three missing phrases need to be completed. Notice that words can be skipped and completed later. For example, to complete the word wagon, the student needs to tap on the three brown boxes: PLA + UST + RUM to spell the Latin word "plaustrum."

As shown in Figure 6.11, the word first appears just to the left of the Go box. Students can then tap the red "X" box to delete the word or the green GO box to submit it. Then just six brown boxes remain at the bottom for sutdents to use to answer the last two questions and to complete the quiz. When all seven words are accurately entered, confetti begins to fall, and a Roman statue appears, explaining "Eugepae!"

When students successfully complete all fifty games in the Easy category, then they can move onto the Medium difficulty games. There are 120 games in the Medium category and a grand total of 1,500 games in the Hard cat-

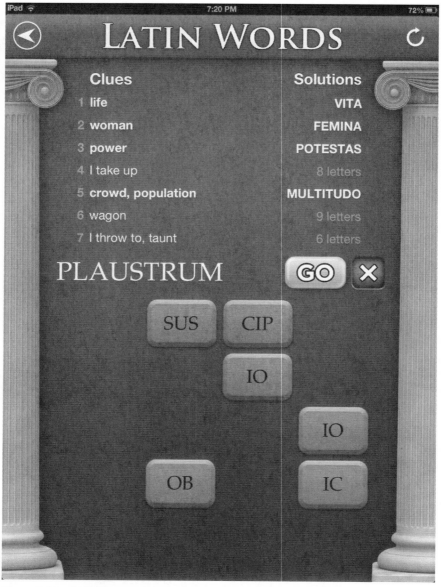

Figure 6.11. Latin's game screen

egory. That is a total of 1,670 games available with this app! Students can learn a great deal during the playing of the games that are associated with this app.

Additional Highly Rated Apps
for Teaching Latin

- SPQR Latin Dictionary and Reader ($6.99)—as described with Latin +
- Latin Flashcards + ($0.99)—come with sample decks containing 1,500 words
- Latin Word Search ($0.99)—another game that students will love

And many more. Mr. Hudson has designed a large number of Latin apps. Most of his are highly rated.

Chinese Language Apps

Fun Chinese—Mandarin Chinese language learning for kids (recommended level: beginner)
Mateo Solares
Website: appocalypse.net/apps/166313-fun-chinese-mandarin-chinese-language-learning-for-
Note: The website listed with iTunes for this app linked only to the Fun English app. This website provides better information about the app.
Cost: Free; also available on Android

The opening screen shows three cute graphics, labeled as Colors, Animals, and Numbers, each leading to a different area of study. Each of those areas opens to a screen, with the following six options, as shown in Figure 6.12:

- Bubbles
- Memory
- Color Search
- Palette
- Two by Two
- Character Match

At the beginning of a Bubbles game, a colored balloon floats onto the screen as a recording provides the Chinese pronunciation for the color. First, a series of two or three balloons emerge; then groups of colors appear, with the recording of only one color. Students gain points by tapping on the correctly colored balloons. Even the smaller balloons should be tapped.

Figure 6.12.   Six options are provided with the Colors lesson.

In the Memory area, six cards drop down on the screen for students to find the three matching pairs. After being tapped, a card turns over to show a color as a recording plays the correct pronunciation for the Chinese word. After all three pairs are matched, a screen shows the time taken to complete the game. Then students are given the option of trying again, continuing to a new level with more cards, or returning to the menu screen. Altogether, there are four levels. This game works best when students are working alone on a single iPad.

For the Color Search, recognizing the colors by hearing becomes more important. A gray and white picture is shown on the screen, for example, a child's bedroom. As students hear a recording of a color in Chinese, they must tap on the item that would most likely have that color. For example, as students hear the Chinese word for "yellow," then they should tap the small toy duck that is in the picture. Similarly, hearing the Chinese word for "red" requires that a heart, which is shown on the wall, should be tapped.

The final Character Match section is the only section that requires recognition of the Chinese symbols that represent colors. Altogether six colors are covered in this section. The characters appear at the top of each screen, and students are to drag those characters past some obstacles and place them over the correct color. Some screens require students to choose the characters in a particular order. This is the hardest area.

On the lower left of the home screen is also a link to a settings area, which offers several options, including, for example, links to an online help page and access to a web page, from which an email can be sent to the designer. To the right of the settings link is a button that provides access to other web pages. A cute little animal in the lower-right corner brings up a page with links to purchase other apps by the designer.

———⁓———

Easy Chinese Writing—yi er san—I write Chinese (recommended level: beginner)
Uniproducts Company, Ltd.
Website: www.iwritechinese.com/
Cost: Free or $1.99

This app comes with the rare rating of five stars! After tapping on the small U.S. flag on the opening screen, users then need to select either simplified or traditional Chinese writing. The following screen provides a choice between learning numbers or nature. Altogether there are ninety Chinese characters or words with the free version, whereas 275 are provided with the paid version.

In addition to the categories of numbers and nature, the paid version has ten more categories: size, family, direction, people, food, transportation, color, fruit, body, and weather. Each category includes seventeen or eighteen individual characters and five compound words (made up of multiple characters put together for a single meaning).

Figure 6.13 shows the number four in the Simplified Chinese. Learning Chinese lettering can be quite intimidating. However, with this app, both the order and the direction that should be taken when writing a letter are clearly indicated. As users trace one of the thin white arrows, a black line appears. When the letter has been correctly traced, a happy face appears on the lower right. The microphone can be tapped to listen to the correct pronunciation. Also an eraser is provided to remove lines that are done incorrectly. There are no indications of an error if the lines are traced in an incorrect order.

The list of number characters starts with the number one, followed by two different characters for the number two; the second one means "both." Subsequently, the numbers are three through ten, then one hundred, thousand, very, many or much, few or little, how many or few, piece or individual, how many or how much, very much/many, eleven, and twenty. In some cases, two symbols are available for a single meaning. This is an excellent app, and the paid version is well worth the investment.

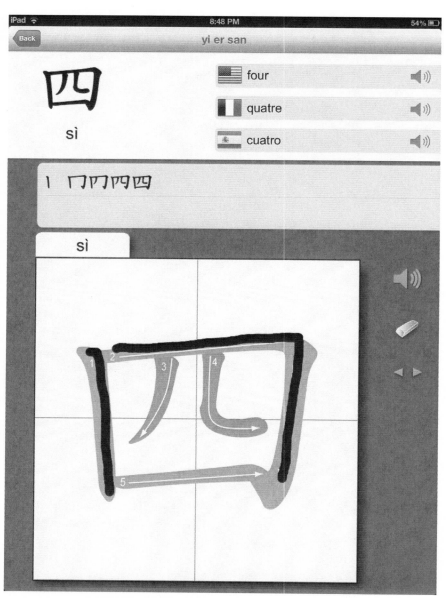

Figure 6.13. Partially traced character

Additional Highly Rated Apps for Teaching Chinese

Learn Chinese Easily
Wan Peng
Cost: Free

This app takes advantage of pictures of objects, with associated recordings. It is highly rated but does include commercials and enticements to buy upgrades.

——⁓⁓⁓——

Learn Chinese (Mandarin)
MindSnacks
Cost: Free

This also is a very highly rated app.

Apps and Lessons for Teaching and Learning American Sign Language (ASL)

Learn American Sign Language (recommended levels: beginner and intermediate)
Selectsoft
Website: www2.selectsoft.com/
Cost: $1.99; also available on Android

A couple of seconds after users open the app, an advertisement for ASL Expressions appears. Users can close the commercial and then make a selection from one of the following nine chapters:

- Introduction
- Meetings & Greetings
- Meeting & Greetings, Part 2
- The Manual Alphabet
- Everyday Communication
- Home & Family
- Emergency Situations
- Emergency Situations, Part 2
- Conclusion

Each chapter has a video of professional sign language interpreter Renee Moore, explaining the various signs, as shown in Figure 6.14. Below each video is the written text of the video so that deaf users can still use this app.

The website below provides a preview of the videos. The videos not only show the correct position of the hands, but they also include discussions about items related to the culture of deaf people. For example, as shown in Figure 8.24, explanations are provided about using a TDD phone, designed for use by the deaf.

Here is an associated video: www.youtube.com/watch?v=vnagB5OHFmk

When you have met a deaf person and have started learning a little bit about the deaf culture and their world, you may want to contact them by telephone. You are probably wondering, "How in the world can I call a deaf person?" or "How do deaf people call each other?"

Let me show you. This is a TDD, or, as it is sometimes called, a TTY. TDD stands for Telecommunications Device for the Deaf. What happens when you are at my house and the phone rings? I pick up the receiver and I say, "Hello?" If there is no answer, I assume there is a deaf person calling me. I take the receiver and I put it in the couplers of my TTY. Then I turn my machine on and start typing across here. What I am typing will print out across the top here. The deaf person is reading this while I am typing. When I'm finished, I type, "GA," which means, "Go ahead." Now it's their turn to have a conversation with me. It's very exciting because most people don't think they can do this. But, if you have a TDD or a TTY as it's called by some, you can call each other and it's wonderful! This is how deaf people call each other and communicate. They have done this for many years but most hearing people have thought, "They don't have telephones."

Figure 6.14. Video and text from chapter 5

———

Baby Sign and Learn (recommended level: beginner)
Baby Sign and Learn
Website: www.babysignandlearn.com/
Cost: Free or $2.99; also available on Android

The Baby Sign and Learn website mentions that the "[h]and-eye coordination [of babies] develops sooner than speech; therefore gesturing is a natural way for babies to communicate." For example, most babies learn to wave good-bye, clap their hands, point to desired objects, and shake their heads to indicate no well before they can speak words. It has been shown that babies as young as eight or nine months old can begin to learn signing. This app provides a fun and engaging way to teach signing to young children.

Unfortunately, this free app comes with only ten words, whereas the paid version includes over three hundred. Obviously, the free version has some low ratings because of the limited number of words, but it provides a good sample of what the paid version has to offer. The opening screen shows five areas that come with this app:

- Watch Signs—Categories: Action Words, Animals, Daily Routines, Feelings and Emotions, Food, Manners and Behavior, and Nature
- Flashcards
- Quiz
- Unlock Signs
- More Apps

Within the Food area, the free app provides only three words: drink, eat, and milk. Figure 6.15 shows a snapshot taken during the animation of the baby girl as she signs the word "fish." The Flashcards and Quiz area are both intuitive and effective ways for strengthening the knowledge of the signs. The last two categories of the home page are ways to buy additional features.

Additional Highly Rated Apps for Teaching ASL

- Sign and Sing is an adorable, free app made by the same company that makes Sign and Learn. However, with this free app, children can learn how to sign the song "Twinkle, Twinkle Little Star."
- 3Strike American Sign Language, by MmpApps, Corp., is free and highly rated.

Figure 6.15. Signing "fish"

Selection of Apps for other Languages

Below is a list of highly rated, free apps for other languages.

Italian			
1.	Learn Italian - MindSnacks	MindSnacks	Free
2.	Learn Italian with busuu!	Busuu Limited	Free
3.	Italian FREE 24/7 Language Learning	24/7 Tutor Inc.	Free or $5.99
4.	Duolingo – Learn Languages for Free	Duolingo	Free
5.	Free Italian English Dictionary	Ascendo, Inc.	Free or $9.99
Japanese			
1.	Learn Japanese Easily	Wan Peng	Free
2.	Learning Japanese	Ronald Timoshenko	Free
3.	Living Language – Japanese for iPad	Random House	Free
4.	Learn Japanese - MindSnacks	MindSnacks	Free
Hebrew			
1.	Learn Hebrew – Free WordPower	Innovative Language Learning	Free
2.	Hebrew Dictionary Free	iThinkdiff	Free
3.	Learn Hebrew – Ma Kore	Online Language Help	Free
Portuguese (* indicates for Brazilian Portuguese)			
1.	Learn Portuguese - MindSnacks	MindSnacks	Free
2.	Learn Portuguese with busuu!	Busuu Limited	Free
3.	O Pequeno Mozart (same app as Little Mozart, discussed in second book of set; switch language in Settings area)	Imagina	Free
4.	*Duolingo – Learn Languages for Free	Duolingo	Free
5.	*Learn Brazilian Portuguese – Free WordPower	Innovative Language Learning	Free
Russian			
1.	Learn Russian	sharkMobi	Free
2.	Learn Russian with busuu!	Busuu Limited	Free
Arabic			
1.	Learn Arabic – iLang	eduGamer	Free
2.	Arabic Dictionary Free	iThinkdiff	Free

Apps Appropriate for the Foreign Language Classroom, but Described Elsewhere

Dictionary.com
Dictionary.com, LLC
Cost: Free

As explained in chapter 4 of this book, this app comes with an area where sentences or paragraphs can be translated into nearly thirty languages. In addition, an option is provided to add a dictionary of a specific language, for an upgrade fee of $1.99.

—⁓—

Booksy: Learn to Read Platform for K–2
Tipitap, Inc.

The description in chapter 4 of this book was selected for teaching reading at the elementary level. However, the books can be purchased in Spanish, so they could be used in Spanish I and II classes.

—⁓—

Logic Advanced
PopAppFactory
Cost: $0.99

This app is discussed in chapter 2 of *The Deuce and a Half iPad*. Users can tap on the Options button to change the language to Spanish, French, Russian, or Ukrainian. This app can be used for practice of and pronunciation of the languages.

—⁓—

High School: PrepZilla Study with Friends Game
gWhiz, LLC
Cost: Free

This app is discussed in chapter 2 of *The Deuce and a Half iPad*. Topics include Spanish.

Websites offering Additional Information on Current Offerings and Trends Concerning Foreign Language Instruction and iPad usage:

- Top Languages to Learn in 2013—August, 2013—thirtysixmonths.com/top-languages-to-learn-in-2013/
- About World Languages Website—Languages in the U.S. Educational System (updated March, 2013)—aboutworldlanguages.com/us-schools

- New York Times article, January 2010—Foreign Languages Fade in Class—Except Chinese—nytimes.com/2010/01/21/education/21 chinese.html?_r=0
- 6 Foreign languages kids should learn, 2010 article from Parents website—www.parents.com/toddlers-preschoolers/development/language/best-foreign-language-for-kids-to-learn/
- iPads in the Foreign Language Classroom—includes links to related research—ipadsforeignlanguage.weebly.com
- EmergingEdTech, December, 2012—Improving Instruction—Increasing Immersion with the iPad in the Foreign Language Classroom—emergingedtech.com/2012/12/improving-instruction-increasing-immersion-with-the-ipad-in-the-foreign-language-classroom/

Reflections on Chapter 6

This chapter discussed or mentioned about seventy-five apps, covering ten languages. That much material could comprise an entire book. However, the apps were all covered within the confines of just one chapter. Only fourteen apps have been discussed more fully. Therefore, the vast majority of the seventy-five apps received only a brief mention. All seventy-five are highly rated, each with a unique value to teachers and students of the specific language. So readers are encouraged to delve further into learning about all the listed apps within each language area.

The chart in the chapter is very revealing concerning the current trends of language instruction in this country. Spanish, French, German, Latin, Chinese, and American Sign Language have been addressed in this chapter, with multiple discussions on specific apps. However, apps are listed for five additional languages: Japanese, Italian, Hebrew, Portuguese, Russian, and Arabic.

Trends may change in upcoming years, but the presence of foreign languages will not disappear. Readers can check the private wiki that is associated with this book to keep up with new language-related apps. I have provided directions for being a member of the wiki in the introduction to this book.

References

1 to 1 EmPOWERedLearning Initiative. (2011). Retrieved from schoolcenter.gcsnc
.com/education/components/scrapbook/default.php?sectiondetailid=328354&link
id=nav-menu-container-4-1436109

Abeling, B. (2012, April 12). Get BIG results from just a few iPads. Retrieved from
wdmtech.wordpress.com/2012/04/29/getting-big-results/

Ackerman, D. (2010, January 27). Should the Apple iPad be considered a computer?
Retrieved from news.cnet.com/8301-17938_105-10442315-1.html

Ashworth, K. (2001). *Caught between the dog and the fireplug, or how to survive public
service*. Washington, DC: Georgetown University Press.

Barseghian, T. (2012, January 23). Study shows algebra iPad app improves scores
in one school. Retrieved from blogs.kqed.org/mindshift/2012/01/study-shows
-algebra-ipad-app-improves-scores-in-one-school/

Bauer, S. W. (2003). *The well-educated mind*. New York: W.W. Norton & Company.

Baugh, D. (2012). iPads improve learning—what the research tells us. Retrieved
from www.digitalcreator.org/dvined/?p=1452

Bloomberg Businessweek. (2010, May 18). Viewpoint: What chief executives really want. Retrieved from www.businessweek.com/innovate/content/may2010/
id20100517_190221.htm

Brian, M. (2012, November 19). Apple's App Store has now seen more than 1 million
approved apps since launch. Retrieved from thenextweb.com/apple/2012/11/19/
apples-app-store-reaches-1-million-approved-app-submissions/

Brown, M. (2012, April 11). The single iPad classroom Retrieved from elementary
edtech.wordpress.com/2012/04/11/the-single-ipad-classroom/

Browning, E. B. (1850). Sonnets from the Portuguese, XLIII. In H. F. Lowry & W. Thorp (Eds.), *An Oxford Anthology of English Poetry* (p. 1059). New York: Oxford University Press.

Butkus, H. (2012, September 7). Tips for the one iPad classroom, and a free iPad rules download! Retrieved from heidisongs.blogspot.com/2012/09/tips-for-one -ipad-classroom-and-free.html

Carroll, L. (1946). *Alice's adventures in wonderland.* Special edition published by Random House, Inc., New York. (Original work published 1898).

Chapla, S. (2011, January 21). Study results: Students benefit from iPads in the classroom. Retrieved from newsinfo.nd.edu/news/18178-study-results-students -benefit-from-ipads-in-the-classroom/

Cherry, S. (2010, April). The iPad is not a computer. Retrieved from spectrum.ieee .org/consumer-electronics/portable-devices/the-ipad-is-not-a-computer

Ciardielio, R. (2012, March 8). Apple launches iPad 3 with much fanfare. Retrieved from smbnation.com/index.php/content/news/entry/apple-launches-ipad-3with -much-fanfare

Daccord, T. (2012, September 27). 5 critical mistakes schools make with iPads (and how to correct them). Retrieved from edudemic.com/2012/09/5-critical-mistakes -schools-ipads-and-correct-them/

della Cava, M. R. (2010, June 6). Does iPad have the magic to bring people to- gether? Retrieved from www.usatoday.com/life/lifestyle/2010-06-07-ipadculture07 _CV_N.htm

Digest of Education Statistics. (2011). Table 16. Retrieved from nces.ed.gov/ programs/digest/d11/tables/dt11_016.asp

Dunn, J. (2012, May 14). A quick guide to managing a classroom full of iPads. Re- trieved from edudemic.com/2012/05/how-to-manage-a-classroom-of-ipads/

Elgan, M. (2010, April 17). Why the iPad is a creativity machine. Retrieved from www.computerworld.com/s/article/9175687/Why_the_iPad_is_a_creativity_ machine

Etherington, D. (2012, September 12). iOS App Store boasts 700K apps, 90% down- loaded every month. Retrieved from techcrunch.com/2012/09/12/ios-app-store -boasts-700k-apps-90-downloaded-every-month/

Faas, R. (2012, August 16). How the iPad is transforming the classroom. Retrieved from www.cultofmac.com/185048/how-the-ipad-is-transforming-the-classroom -back-to-school/

Foley, M. & Hall, D. (2012) MyGrammarLab. Harlow, G.B.: Pearson Education Limited.

Gangwer, T. (2009, December 21). Visual impact, visual teaching. Retrieved from www.visualthesaurus.com/cm/teachersatwork/visual-impact-visual-teaching/

Giacomantonio, L. (2012, September 11). Edmodo reaches 10 million users. Re- trieved from blog.edmodo.com/2012/09/11/edmodo-reaches-10-million-users

Heine, B. (2012, August 17). Why your iPad is almost always the cheapest way to get your textbooks. Retrieved from www.cultofmac.com/185222/why-your-ipad-is-almost-always-the-cheapest-way-to-get-your-textbooks-back-to-school/

Hwang, S. (2012, April 2). iPads in K12 classrooms—empowering students but furthering the learning gap. Retrieved from blog.lib.umn.edu/tel/blog/technology-tools/

Jennings, G. (2012, February 13). Excellent academic results with Trinity's iPad pilot group. Retrieved from ipadpilot.wordpress.com/2012/02/13/excellent-academic-results-with-trinitys-ipad-pilot-group/

Kafka, P. (2011, September 21). What are you doing with your iPad? Playing around, buying apps, watching Netflix. Retrieved from allthingsd.com/20110921/what-are-you-doing-with-your-ipad-playing-around-buying-apps-watching-netflix/

Kerr, D. (2012, September 4). Apple's iPad overtaking PC sales in schools. Retrieved from news.cnet.com/8301-13579_3-57506171-37/apples-ipad-overtaking-pc-sales-in-schools/

Koebler, J. (2011, April 7). Chinese, Japanese language education grows. Retrieved from www.usnews.com/education/blogs/high-school-notes/2011/04/07/chinese-japanese-language-education-grows

Koebler, J. (2011, September 11). More high schools implement iPad programs. Retrieved from www.usnews.com/education/blogs/high-school-notes/2011/09/07/more-high-schools-implement-ipad-programs

Levy, S. (2010, April 3). Apple's iPad: One small step for tablets, one giant leap for personal computers. Retrieved from www.wired.com/reviews/2010/04/pr_ipad_first/

Marmarelli, T., & Ringle, M. (2011). The Reed College iPad study. Retrieved from www.reed.edu/cis/about/ipad_pilot/Reed_ipad_report.pdf

McCracken, H. (2012, September 4). One year later, the iPad is still my favorite computer. Retrieved from techland.time.com/2012/09/04/one-year-later-the-ipad-is-still-my-favorite-computer/

Moats, L. C. (1999). Teaching reading is rocket science: What expert teachers of reading should know and be able to do. Washington, DC: American Federation of Teachers. Retrieved from www.readingrockets.org/articles/researchbytopic/4978/

Partnership for 21st Century Skills. (2012). Organization's home page. Retrieved from www.p21.org/

Pawlowski, Z. (2012). 1 to 1 iPad initiative: Where tradition meets tomorrow. Retrieved from saintcats.org/modules/groups/homepagefiles/cms/1445227/File/SCHS%20iPad%20FAQ.pdf

Pinto, C. (2011, June 29). Showing, not telling: Prezi & Omeka. Retrieved from chronicle.com/blogs/profhacker/showing-not-telling-prezi-omeka/34296

Rhodes, N. C., & Pufahl, I. (2009, November). Foreign language teaching in U.S. schools. Results of a national survey. Retrieved from www.cal.org/projects/Exec%20Summary_111009.pdf

Riconscente, M. (2012). Mobile learning game improves 5th graders' fractions knowledge and attitudes. Retrieved from www.gamedesk.org/projects/motion-math-in-class/

Robinson, K. (2011). Out of our minds. Chichester, West Sussex, UK: Capstone Publishing Ltd.

Rosoff, M. (2011, March 2). Steve Jobs: Tablets are not PCs and our competitors don't get it. Retrieved from articles.businessinsider.com/2011-03-02/tech/29977517_1_pc-market-tablet-market-pc-world

Salerno, M., & Vonhof, M. (2011, December 11). Launching an iPad 1-to-1 program: A primer. Retrieved from thejournal.com/articles/2011/12/14/launching-an-ipad-1-to-1-program-a-primer.aspx

Schuetze, C. (2011, November 23). Textbooks finally take a big leap to digital. Retrieved from www.nytimes.com/2011/11/24/world/americas/schoolwork-gets-swept-up-in-rush-to-go-digital.html?pagewanted=all&_r=0

Shepherd, I., & Reeves, B. (2011, March 1). iPad or iFad—The reality of a paperless classroom. Retrieved from www.acu.edu/technology/mobilelearning/documents/research/ipad-or-ifad.pdf

Sherrin, N. (2008). Oxford Dictionary of Humorous Quotations, Oxford, BC: Oxford University Press, p. 12.

Sinkov, A. (2012, November 8). The new Evernote 5 for iPhone, iPad and iPod Touch. Retrieved from blog.evernote.com/2012/11/08/the-new-evernote-5-for-iphone-ipad-and-ipod-touch/

Stevens, K. (2011, February 4). Using the iPad in ESL learning. Retrieved from voices.yahoo.com/using-ipad-esl-learning-7673184.html

Suffer, J. D., and Gross, D. (2010). Apple unveils the "magical" iPad. Retrieved from articles.cnn.com/2010-01-27/tech/apple.tablet_1_ipad-ibook-tablet?_s=PM:TECH

Swann, A. (2012, July 16). Gamification comes of age. Retrieved from www.forbes.com/sites/gyro/2012/07/16/gamification-comes-of-age/

Tawse, H. (2009, August 22). Using classroom games to achieve your aims. Retrieved from harrytawse56.hubpages.com/hub/Using-Classroom-Games-to-Achieve-Your-Aims

TEDxTalks. (2007, January 6). Sir Ken Robinson: Do schools kill creativity? Retrieved from www.youtube.com/watch?v=iG9CE55wbtY

Van Doren, M. (1944). Liberal education. New York: Henry Holt and Co.

Wakefield, B. (2011, November 13). Apple support communities. Retrieved from discussions.apple.com/thread/3374632?start=105&tstart=0

Walsh, K. (2012, October 24). The importance of iPad insurance in an educational setting. Retrieved from www.emergingedtech.com/2012/10/the-importance-of-ipad-insurance-in-an-educational-setting/

Walsh, K. (2012, December 5). 8 Research findings supporting the benefits of gamification in education. Retrieved from www.emergingedtech.com/2012/12/8-research-findings-supporting-the-benefits-of-gamification-in-education/

Walsh, K. (2012, December 30). The 10 most watched emerging edtech videos of 2012. Retrieved from www.emergingedtech.com/2012/12/the-10-most-watched -emergingedtech-videos-of-2012/

Young, J. R. (2012, January 18). 5 Universities to test bulk-purchasing of e-textbooks in bid to rein in costs. Retrieved from chronicle.com/article/5-Colleges-to-Test/ 130373/

Index

This index is primarily restricted to all apps that are included in this book, even if the app is just briefly mentioned. A few references to hardware and software are also included.

About the Author

Dr. Carrie Thornthwaite is a professor of education at Lipscomb University, in Nashville, Tennessee. In 1997, as she interviewed for the position of director of educational technology, she was asked the question "Are you comfortable with technology?" With her resounding affirmative response, she was hired and has been working ever since to promote the use of technology throughout the education programs.

Her comfort with technology began at a large insurance company in Philadelphia, Pennsylvania, with a single mammoth computer that occupied a large, very cold room. Dr. Thornthwaite wrote programs to run that colossal device. Then, in 1981, she began to write programs on IBM's first desktop computer. One of those devices still sits in the back of a closet in her home.

In 1988, Dr. Thornthwaite began a decade of teaching at a large urban high school in Nashville, Tennessee, where she was elected one year as the school's Teacher of the Year. She taught physics, pre-engineering, and geometry. In 1991, she was the first teacher in the school to have access to the Internet in her classroom. The Internet was very unstable then. When typing an email, going back to correct errors was not possible. The sender had to merely add a comment: "Oops, please ignore the error." By the time Dr. Thornthwaite left the school for the position at Lipscomb, her classroom contained eight computers, which had been used with a variety of software programs.

At the university, Dr. Thornthwaite was responsible for running the department's computer lab. She also designed and taught most of the technology-related courses within the Department of Education. In 2006–2007, she did a great deal of research to support the beginning of an instructional technology master of education program. That program is now provided fully online and "is designed to enhance the classroom experience by using innovative approaches to technology" (2013 Graduate Catalogue). Currently Dr. Thornthwaite teaches solely within the master of education program, almost exclusively through online courses.

Dr. Thornthwaite's published works have been in the areas of technology, cultural diversity, and university–school partnerships. She has provided presentations on a variety of technology topics to dozens of local, national, and international conferences. In addition, she has provided both single- and multiple-day technology workshops. Recently, her workshops have focused on Web 2.0 technologies and the uses of the iPad for teaching and learning in the classroom.